THE ERA OF REFORM
1830–1860

HENRY STEELE COMMAGER

Professor of History
Amherst College

AN ANVIL ORIGINAL

under the general editorship of

LOUIS L. SNYDER

ROBERT E. KRIEGER PUBLISHING COMPANY
MALABAR, FLORIDA
1982

Original Edition   1960
Reprint Edition   1982

Printed and Published by
ROBERT E. KRIEGER PUBLISHING COMPANY, INC.
KRIEGER DRIVE
MALABAR, FLORIDA 32950

Printed in the United States of America

Library of Congress Cataloging in Publication Data

Main entry under title:

The Era of reform, 1830-1860.

  Reprint. Originally published: Princeton, N.J.:
Van Nostrand, 1960. (An Anvil original)
  Bibliography: p.
  Includes index.
1. Social reformers—United States—Addressess,
essays, lectures. 2. United States—Social conditions—
To 1865. I. Commager, Henry Steele, 1902-
HN64.E68   1982   303.4'84   82-15190
ISBN 0-89874-498-9   AACR2

TABLE OF CONTENTS

3

IV WOMEN'S RIGHTS

V ECONOMIC REFORM

VI LAND REFORM

VII EDUCATION

VIII HUMANITARIANISM

IX THE PEACE CRUSADE

CONCLUSION

INTRODUCTION

"It was now the day of ideals in every camp. The general restlessness was as intense among reflecting Conservatives as among reflecting Liberals; and those who looked to the past agreed with those who looked to the future, in energetic dissatisfaction with a sterile present. . . . A great wave of humanity, of benevolence, of desire for improvement . . . poured itself among all who had the faculty for large and disinterested thinking." John Morley was describing Richard Cobden's England (and his own, as well) but what he wrote applied with even greater force to the America of the Middle Period of the nineteenth century. It was a day of universal reform —a day when almost every man you met might draw a plan for a new society or a new government from his pocket; a day of infinite hope and infinite discontent. Every institution was called before the bar of reason, and of sentiment, too: the church, the state, the law, the army, the family, property—and required to justify itself. Nothing was immune, nothing was sacred, nothing was taken for granted, nothing but the right of inquiry. "A restless, prying, conscientious criticism broke out in the most unexpected quarters. . . . Am I not a too protected person? Is there not a wide disparity between the lot of me and the lot of thee, my poor brother, my poor sister?" So asked Emerson, the cow from which they all drew their milk. "In the history of the world the doctrine of reform never had such scope as at the present hour." It is Emerson, again—"We are to revise the whole of our social structure—the state, the school, religion, marriage, trade, science, and explore the foundations in our own nature." It is this moral fundamentalism, this radical comprehensiveness, that most sharply distinguishes the reform era of the Middle Period from the other major reform eras of our history—the Revolution, the Populist-Progressive period, and the New Deal. These were, for the most part, political and constitutional; they were nationalistic and even parochial; they were secular

7

and practical; the last two of them, at least, were op-
portunistic and almost without benefit of philosophy.
But the reform movement of the generation of Emerson
and Theodore Parker, Horace Mann and Margaret Fuller,
had a very different character. Let us examine that character.

First, this reform movement was, to an astonishing
degree, the product of philosophy—or at least of a
dominant and pervasive view of the nature of Man
and the relation of Man to Nature and to God. That
philosophy we call Transcendentalism. It assumed that
there were great moral truths that are *a priori*, and that
transcend mere sensational proof. The most important of
these—if there can be a hierarchy of truth—were that
God is benevolent, Nature beneficent, and Man divine.
These were not new ideas—after all they had been widely
accepted during the Enlightenment; what was new was
their subjective and *a priori* authentication. And if these
moral principles were, in reality, true, then it followed that
any secular departure from them was contrary to God's
purpose with man. If Man was divine, and mankind
perfectable, then it was unspeakably wicked that a man's
body should be confined in slavery, his mind clouded
by ignorance, his soul corrupted by superstition or by sin.
Let there be light! Let us restore men to that divinity with
which God endowed them. Let us bring freedom to the
slave, learning to the ignorant, enlightenment to the
superstitious, prosperity to the poor, health to the sick
and the crippled; let us give to women, to children, to
workingmen, to the perishing and the dangerous classes,
all of those rights and privileges and opportunities and
benefactions that God and Nature intended they should
enjoy! As Emerson so well put it: "The power which
is at once spring and regulator in all efforts of reform
is the conviction that there is an infinite worthiness in
man, which appears at the call of worth, and that all
particular reforms are the removing of some impediment."

"The removing of some impediment!" What is man
born for but to be a re-former—to remove impediments,
to recast institutions, to make over man himself? God
would not have made Nature benevolent and Man divine
if He had not intended perfection. It could be achieved
—it would be achieved, now.

The reform movement, then, was designed to harmonize man with the moral order, and it quickly took on the character of a moral crusade. More, it took on the character of a religious crusade; it is the only one of our major reform movements that had this character, and the only one where the clergy provided not only inspiration but leadership. The Revolutionary leaders were moral, but rarely pious; they distrusted organized religion and invoked God as they invoked Nature, as an impersonal part of a cosmic system with which they wished to be in harmony. And as for the New Deal, even its most high-minded architects did not argue the Divinity of Man, or look to moral regeneration. And who was the Channing of the Revolutionary era, who the Parker of the Roosevelt Revolution? But what would the reform movement of this middle period be without its phalanxes of clergy: Emerson, Channing, Parker, Ripley, Pierpont, Hedge, Higginson, Brownson, Weld, Sam Jo May and James Freeman Clark, and a score of others? And what would it have been without their disciples, without Bronson Alcott and Margaret Fuller who looked to Emerson; and Dorothea Dix and Wendell Phillips who depended on Channing; and S. G. Howe and Horace Mann who drew strength from Parker; without the evangelical fervor of a Theodore Weld and the piety of the Tappan brothers, and the moral fervor of the daughter of the Reverend Lyman Beecher and the wife of the Reverend Calvin Stowe!

We are so familiar with the Transcendentalist philosophy of this reform movement, with its religious impetus and its clerical leadership, that we are tempted to take it for granted. But it is important to note that Transcendentalism did not sponsor reform in Germany, or in England or, for that matter, among the Kantian idealists of Vermont: James Marsh, who has some right to speak for them, dismissed "the whole of Boston Transcendentalism" as "a superficial affair." In Britain, indeed, it was the Utilitarians and the Rationalists—the heirs of John Locke—who were the reformers. Perhaps the simplest explanation of the otherwise mysterious failure of Utilitarianism to play any significant role in America is that in America Utilitarianism was called Transcendentalism. Never was the resourcefulness of the American better revealed than in his ability, in one generation, to work a revolution out of the philosophy of Locke and, in the next, out of a philosophy that repudiated Locke.

A third characteristic of the reform movement of this era is its comprehensiveness. *Every* institution was called upon to show its credentials, and to justify its course of conduct—the great and the trivial alike, the institution of the State or the practice of shaving, the institution of the Church, or the eating of meat, the institution of marriage or the wearing of beards! In our day most reformers are content with a single crusade, but the reformers of the 'thirties were, most of them, "universal" reformers. Bronson Alcott proposed a Club for the Study and Diffusion of Ideas and Tendencies Proper to the Nineteenth Century; Robert Owen called a World Convention to Emancipate the Human Race from Ignorance, Poverty, Division, and Misery; Garrison proclaimed that "the world was his country and his countrymen all mankind" and John Humphrey Noyes—another of the universal reformers—reported that Garrison's mind "was heaving with the subject of Holiness and the Kingdom of God, and he would devote himself to them as soon as he could get anti-slavery off his hands." As soon as he came to Boston, young Theodore Parker issued a call for a "council of Reformers" to discuss "the General Principles of Reform" and the means of promoting them, and when the Council duly met it spent six hours discussing "All the Holy Principles of Reform." Nor was this universality verbal only. Parker championed religious freedom, woman's rights, the cause of labor, penal and prison reform, peace, and abolition. Wendell Phillips took on antislavery, woman's rights, labor reform, and money reform. Horace Greeley was interested in Fourierism, free land, the rights of labor and of women, purity in politics, peace, penal reform, temperance, and at least a hearing for spiritualism, Grahamism, and phrenology. The New York philanthropist Gerrit Smith began as an anti-Mason, took up vegetarianism and dress reform and temperance, championed the cause of the Greeks and the Irish, settled poor whites and Negroes on his Adirondack lands, advocated woman suffrage, and in the end concentrated on antislavery and helped finance the Kansas crusade and John Brown.

With all this there was, inevitably, an interlocking directorate of reformers. One good cause always led to another, and each of the reformers had to help out all the others if he expected their help in his particular crusade. Besides, all the reforms were interrelated, all part of a larger moral pattern; neither salvation nor divinity was divisable.

Fourth, this reform crusade, again in contrast to the Revolution and to the great reforms of the twentieth century, was highly individualistic. Given its original philosophy, that was inevitable, for Transcendentalism, after all, vindicated private truth and private salvation. The characteristic figure of this era was the Come-Outer, who had always in mind the admonition by Lowell:

> They are slaves who dare not be
> In the right with two or three

And if it was impossible to get two or three, one would do. Thoreau was no Come-Outer, not consciously any-way, but Walden Pond was nevertheless something of a symbol for his generation of New England intellectuals. Yet for all their individualism, these reformers were al-ways organizing and holding meetings—across state boundaries, even across the ocean. What a passion they had for Conventions—Antislavery and Woman's Rights, and Peace, and Temperance, and a dozen others. They organized Utopian communities, too, though few of these worked, and fewer still survived. But no one was asked, or expected, to subordinate his mind (or to still his voice) to the common will; there was unlimited discussion and an unlimited right of secession. It is a wonder that they ever got anything done, what with all the societies to organize and letters to write and conventions to attend and speeches to deliver, and what with the whole of society to reform, and that overnight! But they did. They had the Victorian capacity for work, which we have lost; they worked prodigiously; they wrote voluminously; they talked in-cessantly; they accomplished twice as much as any subsequent generation.

Fifth, the obverse side of this passionate individualism and voluntarism is that the reform movement, in marked contrast with the other major reforms, and with the contemporary English reform activity, was non-political.

It did not boast a Jefferson or a Hamilton, a Bryan or a Theodore Roosevelt, a Franklin D. Roosevelt or a Henry Wallace; it did not even have anyone in public life of the stature of Lord Brougham. This indifference to, or positive repudiation of, politics was rooted in philosophy; after all, if you are going to obey Higher Law you must be prepared (like Thoreau, like Garrison, like Parker) to get along without mere secular law. Besides, of what use to rely on government? It was like expecting a criminal to dispense justice! Was not government itself leagued with the forces of unrighteousness? It was the State that fought wars; it was the State that supported slavery; it was the State that subjected women to monstrous subordination and exploited little children. As Lowell told them it was a case of

> Right forever on the scaffold,
> wrong forever on the throne.

So, Thoreau proclaimed the moral duty of civil disobedience; Garrison publicly burned the Constitution; Parker and Higginson attacked the Court House; Emerson read the Fugitive Slave law and wrote in his Journal, "This filthy enactment was made in the nineteenth century, by men who could read and write. I will not obey it, by God!"; and Lowell—and others—seceded from the Mexican War.

There were, to be sure, exceptions to this repudiation of politics. Robert Owen and Frances Wright helped organize a Workingman's Party; George Bancroft was ceaselessly active in politics, and Horace Greeley, too. It says much for the futility of reliance on party that the Workingman's Party petered out in a year or so, and that Bancroft could be an ardent Democrat and Greeley an ardent Whig, and neither have anything much to show for their party ardors. Some of the reformers, to be sure, had to work through the machinery of the State: Horace Mann and his colleagues who fought for public schools; the gallant Dorothea Dix who enlisted the sympathy of state legislators on behalf of the desperate and the perishing classes of society; even the land reformers, who finally pushed a Homestead Act through Congress. But on the whole, reform was not political, and politics was not reformist.

A sixth characteristic of this reform movement is that it was fanatical without being violent, and radical without being revolutionary. Notwithstanding agitation as extreme as any on the European continent, and attacks on established institutions as vehement, the United States (like England) escaped the uprisings so widespread on the European continent in the 'forties. No governments were toppled, not even in Rhode Island; no tyrants were unhorsed; there were no barricades in the streets, and no soldiers to ride down desperate mobs. If the American reform was a revolution, it was the most sedate of revolutions, conducted with weapons that were all moral and intellectual, wielded by the most dignified group of agitators in history. Those who were not clergymen were men of letters; one sometimes feels that a degree from Harvard or a clerical collar was a prerequisite to admission to the ranks of the insurgents. There were, to be sure, isolated instances of violence: Thoreau defied a tax-collector; Garrison burned the Constitution; Parker excited forcible nullification of the Fugitive Slave Act; the long-suffering tenants of Rensselaerwyck killed a sheriff; and poor Thomas Dorr led a pop-gun rebellion. All this furnished rich material for poems and sermons and tracts by the hundred, but it adds up to less violence than any self-respecting metropolis boasts in a single year in our own day. Yet there is this to be said of the reformers—the Phillipses and Parkers, the Tappans and Welds, the Howes, and the Dorrs—that peaceable as they were, they meant business.

The fate of Thomas Dorr, who was given a life sentence for treason and released the next year, suggests a parallel characteristic: as the reformers did not themselves use violence, they were not the victims of violence. They kept—most of them—their jobs, their pulpits, their college posts, their editorial chairs, their popularity on the lyceum circuit. Nobody boycotted Emerson; Parker preached to three thousand parishioners on a Sunday; Greeley managed to sell a few copies of the *Tribune;* Horace Mann went to Congress, and so did Gerrit Smith; Samuel Gridley Howe married a New York heiress, and the Tappans kept their social position and their money. Harriet Martineau could write on The Martyr Age in the United States, and many of the reformers longed for martyrdom, but few achieved it. Again there were exceptions, especially among the Abolitionists: the gallant Elijah Lovejoy comes to mind, and perhaps John Brown, and some others, reckless agitators who openly defied public opinion, headstrong abolitionists who invaded the South, or fugitive slaves who were caught and sent back to slavery. Yet the interesting fact is that while there was a radical movement, and a radical philosophy, there was no counter conservative movement or conservative philosophy. What Horace Mann and Wendell Phillips and Margaret Fuller had to deal with was inertia rather than resistance; certainly it was not counterrevolution.

An eighth characteristic of the reform movement was its regional and sectional character. Like the literature of the day, it was, to an extraordinary degree, a flowering of New England. It is true that New York made important contributions, especially the "burnt-over" region, and that Ohio, especially the Western Reserve, was not without influence. But no one who studies either the philosophy or the leadership of the movement can mistake its sharp New England flavor. Call the roll of the leaders: Emerson, its philosopher; Channing and Parker, its theologians; Horace Mann, its educator, and with him Henry Barnard and John Carter; Catherine Beecher and Margaret Fuller and Mary Lyons and Emma Willard, champions of woman's rights; William Ladd and Elihu Burritt, workers in the vineyards of peace; the Chevalier Howe and Dorothea Dix and Charles Loring Brace in humanitarian reform; the abolitionists Garrison and Phillips, Theodore Weld and Horace Greeley, and even Lovejoy himself. The literary spokesmen, too, almost all bore the New England stamp: Emerson and Thoreau, Lowell and Whittier, Bryant and Greeley; it is suggestive that the other major literary figures of that day—Irving and Cooper, Poe and Simms, and Melville —were for the most part indifferent to the appeal of reform.

What is equally impressive, but not equally puzzling, is that the South was almost wholly untouched by reform, not only by the currents of antislavery—that was to be expected—but even by those of education and humanitarianism. The explanation is not difficult. To Southerners, painfully sensitive to attacks on their peculiar institution, all "isms" were alike, and all obnoxious: abolitionism, feminism, Utopianism, Unitarianism, Republicanism, equalitarianism, humanitarianism. Thus the Richmond *Enquirer* wrote of the campaign of 1856 that if the Republicans had their way the "isms" of "free society, lectures against marriage, licentious philansteries, free love saloons, Mormon states and Quaker villages" would spread all over the South. Or, as one writer in *De Bow's Review* put it in urging exclusive reliance on the Bible and Aristotle: "Books written in the whole range of moral science, if not written by Southern authors, within the last twenty or thirty years, inculcate abolition either directly or indirectly. If written before that time, even by Southern authors, they are likely to be as absurd and as dangerous as the Declaration of Independence, or the Virginia Bill of Rights." In short the Southern attitude was not unlike that of some of our professional red-baiters today: whatever Northern liberals said or did was pernicious, because it was contaminated at its source. And, given their assumptions about the necessity and the sanctity of slavery, Southerners were, of course, right, for slavery could not stand the open mind, and education and humanitarian reform threatened to open minds.

Ninth, along with regionalism, went cosmopolitanism. The currents of reform did not seep below the Mason-Dixon line, but they flowed across the Atlantic like some Gulf Stream, and provided a common climate for the United States and Britain. The reform movement of this generation was, in fact, Anglo-American, it was even international. Quakers and Unitarians, in their determination to do good, ignored national boundaries; labor leaders and land reformers carried on their agitation with equal fervor in Manchester and in New York. The antislavery movement had its real beginnings in England, and its greatest triumphs. The struggle for woman's rights, for temperance, for peace, were all joint enterprises. Penal reform owed more to Bentham and Romilly and Elizabeth Fry than to any American, and Bentham could write to President Jackson that "I am more of a United States man than an Englishman." Educational reform had its real origins in Swiss cantons and German states where Pestalozzi and Fellenberg and Wehrli and Froebel fixed

the patterns that Horace Mann and Henry Barnard and
Calvin Stowe tried to copy. The Utopian movement,
originally inspired by an America which seemed Nature's
Utopia, had its formal origins in England and France,
and many of the leaders of American Utopianism—
"Mother" Ann Lee, founder of the Shakers, and Robert
Owen of New Harmony and Frances Wright of Nashoba
—were from the British Isles, while phalanxes were
modelled on the plans of Charles Fourier, and Icaria on
those drawn by Étienne Cabet, and the romantic Oleana
sprang from the musical bow of Ole Bull.

Finally, reform was one aspect of romanticism, as
was Transcendentalism for that matter, for what is more
romantic than the cultivation of individual truth and
individual salvation? Romanticism did not so much
prescribe particular reforms as infuse the spirit of reform.
It found expression in a sentimental, and philosophical,
attitude toward Nature—we can see it in the paintings of
Bierstadt or Church, in Emerson's famous Address, and
in Thoreau's Walden; and in the sentimental attitude
toward women and children, and primitive peoples as
well. It is possible that the sentimentalizing of the slave
by Stephen Foster or Harriet Beecher Stowe made more
converts to abolition than the arguments of a Garrison
or a Parker. Romanticism was intimately connected with
the new humanitarianism—the attack on capital punishment, the reform of the penal code, the tender concern
for the blind and the deaf, the sick and the feeble-minded,
the more compassionate treatment of animals, children,
felons, and sailors. It informed alike the antislavery poems
of Whittier, the annual reports on education by Horace
Mann, and Herman Melville's *Mardi*.

Yet it is important to note that romanticism did not
necessarily inspire or encourage reform. In much of
Europe it had just the contrary effect, and in the American South, too, where it nourished the myth that slavery
was a blessing to the blacks and that the plantation
system was but an improvement on medieval chivalry.
It is proper to inquire why romanticism worked one way
in Germany or England or the American South, and
another way in New England and Ohio and New York.
Is this just another example of the resourcefulness of
Americans, like their ability to make Transcendentalism do

the work of Utilitarianism? To some extent it is. But there is more to it than that. For it can be argued that Yankees read the meaning of romanticism more accurately than Carlyle or Hegel or Viollet-le-Duc or, for that matter, John Pendleton Kennedy or George Fitzhugh. Where European and Southern reactionaries read into it the picturesque, the Gothic, the aristocratic, and the traditional, northern Americans read into it the goodness of Nature, the divinity of man, and the infinite promise of the future. James Fenimore Cooper put it well in an observation by his "traveling bachelor":

> The moral feeling with which a man of sentiment and knowledge looks upon the plains of your (Eastern) hemisphere, is connected with recollections; here it should be mingled with his hopes. The same effort of the mind is as equal to the one as to the other. . . . But the speculator on moral things can enjoy a satisfaction here that he who wanders over the plains of Greece will seek in vain. The pleasure of the latter . . . is unavoidably tinged with melancholy regrets, while here all that reason allows may be hoped on behalf of man.

That might indeed be the epitaph of the great reform movement of the Middle Period, all the more appropriate because wrung, as it were, from one of the few major literary figures who had no use for reform or reformers: "All that reason allows may be hoped on behalf of man."

I

THE PHILOSOPHY OF REFORM

— Reading No. 1 —

THOMAS JEFFERSON: ALL EYES ARE OPENED TO THE RIGHTS OF MAN, 1826[1]

Jefferson belongs to the Revolutionary generation, but, living to 1826, he forms a link between the age of the Founding Fathers and the Age of Reform. This letter to Mayor Weightman, written less than two weeks before his death, expresses with characteristic eloquence that buoyant faith in man, in liberty, and in progress which has made Jefferson the patron saint of American democracy.

✔   ✔   ✔

Respected Sir, The kind invitation I receive from you, on the part of the citizens of the city of Washington, to be present with them at their celebration on the fiftieth anniversary of American Independence, as one of the surviving signers of an instrument pregnant with our own, and the fate of the world, is most flattering to myself, and heightened by the honorable accompaniment

[1] From Paul L. Ford, ed., *The Writings of Thomas Jefferson* (New York, 1899) X, 390-92.

proposed for the comfort of such a journey. It adds sensibly to the sufferings of sickness, to be deprived by it of a personal participation in the rejoicings of that day. But acquiescence is a duty, under circumstances not placed among those we are permitted to control. I should, indeed, with peculiar delight, have met and exchanged there congratulations personally with the small band, the remnant of that host of worthies, who joined with us on that day, in the bold and doubtful election we were to make for our country, between submission or the sword; and to have enjoyed with them the consolatory fact, that our fellow citizens, after half a century of experience and prosperity, continue to approve the choice we made. May it be to the world, what I believe it will be, (to some parts sooner, to others later, but finally to all,) the signal of arousing men to burst the chains under which monkish ignorance and superstition had persuaded them to bind themselves, and to assume the blessings and security of self-government. That form which we have substituted, restores the free right to the unbounded exercise of reason and freedom of opinion. All eyes are opened, or opening, to the rights of man. The general spread of the light of science has already laid open to every view the palpable truth, that the mass of mankind has not been born with saddles on their backs, nor a favored few booted and spurred, ready to ride them legitimately, by the grace of God. These are grounds of hope for others. For ourselves, let the annual return of this day forever refresh our recollections of these rights, and an undiminished devotion to them.

I will ask permission here to express the pleasure with which I should have met my ancient neighbors of the city of Washington and its vicinities, with whom I passed so many years of a pleasing social intercourse; an intercourse which so much relieved the anxieties of the public cares, and left impressions so deeply engraved in my affections, as never to be forgotten. With my regret that ill health forbids me the gratification of an acceptance, be pleased to receive for yourself, and those for whom you write, the assurance of my highest respect and friendly attachments.

—THOMAS JEFFERSON, Letter to Roger C. Weightman, June 24, 1826.

— Reading No. 2 —

RALPH WALDO EMERSON: MAN THE REFORMER, 1841 [2]

Much of the English reform movement grew out of Utilitarianism; much of the American reform movement from Transcendentalism. Although in the Old World Transcendentalism lent itself to the search for individual salvation, and even to reaction, in the United States its principles—if we can use that term at all in relation to a body of ideas so amorphous—inspired a crusade for progress, humanitarianism, and equality. Emerson was not himself active in reform, but he was at once the inspiration and the historian of much of the reform movement, particularly its New England manifestations. The essay on "Man the Reformer" was written in 1841.

✔   ✔   ✔

MAN THE REFORMER

In the history of the world the doctrine of Reform had never such scope as at the present hour. Lutherans, Herrnhuters, Jesuits, Monks, Quakers, Knox, Wesley, Swedenborg, Bentham, in their accusations of society, all respected something,—church or state, literature or history, domestic usages, the market town, the dinner table, coined money. But now all these and all things else hear the trumpet, and must rush to judgment,—Christianity, the laws, commerce, schools, the farm, the laboratory; and not a kingdom, town, statute, rite, calling, man, or woman, but is threatened by the new spirit.

What if some of the objections whereby our institutions are assailed are extreme and speculative, and the reformers tend to idealism? That only shows the ex-

[2] From R. W. Emerson, *Nature, Addresses, and Lectures,* v.d.

travagance of the abuses which have driven the mind into the opposite extreme. It is when your facts and persons grow unreal and fantastic by too much falsehood that the scholar flies for refuge to the world of ideas, and aims to recruit and replenish nature from that source. Let ideas establish their legitimate sway again in society, let life be fair and poetic, and the scholars will gladly be lovers, citizens, and philanthropists.

It will afford no security from the new ideas that the old nations, the laws of centuries, the property and institutions of a hundred cities, are built on other foundations. The demon of reform has a secret door into the heart of every lawmaker, of every inhabitant of every city. The fact that a new thought and hope have dawned in your breast should apprize you that in the same hour a new light broke in upon a thousand private hearts. That secret which you would fain keep,—as soon as you go abroad, lo! there is one standing on the doorstep to tell you the same. There is not the most bronzed and sharpened money-catcher who does not, to your consternation almost, quail and shake the moment he hears a question prompted by the new ideas. We thought he had some semblance of ground to stand upon, that such as he at least would die hard; but he trembles and flees. Then the scholar says, "Cities and coaches shall never impose on me again; for behold every solitary dream of mine is rushing to fulfilment. That fancy I had, and hesitated to utter because you would laugh,—the broker, the attorney, the market-man are saying the same thing. Had I waited a day longer to speak, I had been too late. Behold, State Street thinks, and Wall Street doubts, and begins to prophesy!"

It cannot be wondered at that this general inquest into abuses should arise in the bosom of society, when one considers the practical impediments that stand in the way of virtuous young men. The young man, on entering life, finds the way to lucrative employments blocked with abuses. The ways of trade are grown selfish to the borders of theft, and supple to the borders (if not beyond the borders) of fraud. The employments of commerce are not intrinsically unfit for a man, or less genial to his faculties; but these are now in their general course so vitiated by derelictions and abuses at which all connive that it requires more vigor and resources than can be expected of every young man to right himself in them; he is lost in them; he cannot move hand or foot in them. Has he genius and virtue? the less does he find them fit for him to grow in, and if he would thrive in them, he must sacrifice all the brilliant dreams of boyhood and youth as dreams; he must forget the prayers of his childhood and must take on him the harness of routine and obsequiousness. If not so minded, nothing is left him but to begin the world anew, as he does who puts the spade into the ground for food. We are all implicated of course in this charge; it is only necesssary to ask a few questions as to the progress of the articles of commerce from the fields where they grew, to our houses, to become aware that we eat and drink and wear perjury and fraud in a hundred commodities. . . .

The idea which now begins to agitate society has a wider scope than our daily employments, our households, and the institutions of property. We are to revise the whole of our social structure, the State, the school, religion, marriage, trade, science, and explore their foundations in our own nature; we are to see that the world not only fitted the former men, but fits us, and to clear ourselves of every usage which has not its roots in our own mind. What is a man born for but to be a Reformer, a Remaker of what man has made; a renouncer of lies; a restorer of truth and good, imitating that great Nature which embosoms us all, and which sleeps no moment on an old past, but every hour repairs herself, yielding us every morning a new day, and with every pulsation a new life? Let him renounce everything which is not true to him, and put all his practices back on their first thoughts, and do nothing for which he has not the whole world for his reason. If there are inconveniences and what is called ruin in the way, because we have so enervated and maimed ourselves, yet it would be like dying of perfumes to sink in the effort to re-attach the deeds of every day to the holy and mysterious recesses of life.

The power which is at once spring and regulator in all efforts of reform is the conviction that there is an infinite worthiness in man, which will appear at the call of worth, and that all particular reforms are the removing of some impediment. Is it not the highest duty that man should be honored in us? I ought not to allow any man because he has broad lands to feel that he is rich in my presence. I ought to make him feel that I can do without his riches, that I cannot be bought,—neither by comfort, neither by pride,—and though I be utterly penniless, and receiving bread from him, that he is the poor man beside me. And if, at the same time, a woman or a child discovers a sentiment of piety, or a juster way of thinking than mine, I ought to confess it by my respect and obedience, though it go to alter my whole way of life. . . .

Let our affection flow out to our fellows; it would operate in a day the greatest of all revolutions. It is better to work on institutions by the sun than by the wind. The State must consider the poor man, and all voices must speak for him. Every child that is born must have a just chance for his bread. Let the amelioration in our laws of property proceed from the concession of the rich, not from the grasping of the poor. Let us begin by habitual imparting. Let us understand that the equitable rule is that no one should take more than his share, let him be ever so rich. Let me feel that I am to be a lover. I am to see to it that the world is the better for me, and to find my reward in the act. Love would put a new face on this weary old world in which we dwell as pagans and enemies too long, and it would warm the heart to see how fast the vain diplomacy of statesmen, the impotence of armies, and navies, and lines of defence, would be superseded by this unarmed child. Love will creep where it cannot go, will accomplish that by imperceptible methods, —being its own lever, fulcrum, and power,—which force could never achieve. Have you not seen in the woods, in a late autumn morning, a poor fungus of mushroom,— a plant without any solidity, nay, that seemed nothing but a soft mush or jelly,—by its constant, total, and inconceivably gentle pushing, manage to break its way up through the frosty ground, and actually to lift a hard crust on its head? It is the symbol of the power of kindness. The virtue of this principle in human society in application to great interests is absolute and forgotten. Once or twice in history it has been tried in illustrious instances, with signal success. This great, overgrown, dead

Christendom of ours still keeps alive at least the name
of a lover of mankind. But one day all men will be
lovers; and every calamity will be dissolved in the universal sunshine.

— Reading No. 3 —

RALPH WALDO EMERSON: THE NEW ENGLAND REFORMERS, 1844[3]

*For reasons never satisfactorily explained, New Eng-
land, and particularly eastern Massachusetts, was the
heart of the American reform movement. From this region came Emerson, the philosopher of the movement;
Parker, its preacher; Phillips, its orator; Channing, its
benign presence; Margaret Fuller, its Minerva; Horace
Mann, its educator; Samuel G. Howe, its crusader;
George Ripley, its Utopian practitioner; Sumner, its poli-
tician; and many others. The various activities that went
to make up the reform movement had their absurd as
well as their solemn and sincere aspects; in this memo-
rable essay Emerson writes sympathetically of the first,
and appreciatively of the second.*

✔   ✔   ✔

What a fertility of projects for the salvation of the
world! One apostle thought all men should go to farming,
and another that no man should buy or sell, that the use
of money was the cardinal evil; another that the mischief was in our diet, that we eat and drink damnation.
These made unleavened bread and were foes to the death

[3] From R. W. Emerson, *Essays, Second Series* (v. ed.; v.d.).

to fermentation. It was in vain urged by the housewife that God made yeast as well as dough and loves fermentation just as dearly as he loves vegetation, that fermentation develops the saccharine element in the grain and makes it more palatable and more digestible. No; they wish the pure wheat, and will die but it shall not ferment. Stop, dear Nature, these incessant advances of thine; let us scotch these ever-rolling wheels! Others attacked the system of agriculture, the use of animal manures in farming, and the tyranny of man over brute nature; these abuses polluted his food. The ox must be taken from the plow and the horse from the cart, the hundred acres of the farm must be spaded, and the man must walk, wherever boats and locomotives will not carry him. Even the insect world was to be defended—that had been too long neglected, and a society for the protection of ground worms, slugs, and mosquitoes was to be incorporated without delay. With these appeared the adepts of homeopathy, of hydropathy, of mesmerism, of phrenology, and their wonderful theories of the Christian miracles! Others assailed particular vocations, as that of the lawyer, that of the merchant, of the manufacturer, of the clergyman, of the scholar. Others attacked the institution of marriage as the fountain of social evils. Others devoted themselves to the worrying of churches and meetings for public worship, and the fertile forms of antinomianism among the elder puritans seemed to have their match in the plenty of the new harvest of reform.

With this din of opinion and debate there was a keener scrutiny of institutions and domestic life than any we had known; there was sincere protesting against existing evils, and there were changes of employment dictated by conscience.

There was in all the practical activities of New England for the last quarter of a century [1815-1840] a gradual withdrawal of tender consciences from the social organizations. There is observable throughout, the contest between mechanical and spiritual methods, but with a steady tendency of the thoughtful and virtuous to a deeper belief and reliance on spiritual facts.

In politics, for example, it is easy to see the progress of dissent. The country is full of rebellion; the country is full of kings. Hands off! let there be no control and no

interference in the administration of the affairs of this
kingdom of me. Hence the growth of the doctrine and
of the party of free trade and the willingness to try that
experiment in the face of what appear incontestable facts.
I confess the motto of the *Globe* newspaper is so attrac-
tive to me that I can seldom find much appetite to read
what is below it in its columns: "The world is governed
too much." So the country is frequently affording solitary examples of resistance to the government, solitary
nullifiers who throw themselves on their reserved rights;
nay, who have reserved all their rights; who reply to the
assessor and to the clerk of court that they do not know
the State, and embarrass the courts of law by nonjuring
and the commander-in-chief of the militia by nonresist-
ance.

The same disposition to scrutiny and dissent appeared
in civil, festive, neighborly, and domestic society. A restless, prying, conscientious criticism broke out in unexpected quarters. Who gave me the money with which I
bought my coat? Why should professional labor and that
of the countinghouse be paid so disproportionately to the
labor of the porter and wood sawyer? This whole business of trade gives me to pause and think, as it constitutes false relations between men, inasmuch as I am
prone to count myself relieved of any responsibility to
behave well and nobly to that person whom I pay with
money; whereas, if I had not that commodity, I should
be put on my good behavior in all companies, and man
would be a benefactor to man, as being himself his only
certificate that he had a right to those aids and services
which each asked of the other. Am I not too protected
a person? Is there not a wide disparity between the lot
of me and the lot of thee, my poor brother, my poor
sister? Am I not defrauded of my best culture in the loss
of those gymnastics which manual labor and the emer-
gencies of poverty constitute? I find nothing healthful or
exalting in the smooth conventions of society; I do not
like the close air of saloons. I begin to suspect myself to
be a prisoner, though treated with all this courtesy and
luxury. I pay a destructive tax in my conformity.

The same insatiable criticism may be traced in the
efforts for the reform of education. The popular education has been taxed with a want of truth and nature. It

was complained that an education to things was not given. We are students of words; we are shut up in schools, and colleges, and recitation rooms, for ten or fifteen years, and come out at last with a bag of wind, a memory of words, and do not know a thing. We cannot use our hands, or our legs, or our eyes, or our arms. We do not know an edible root in the woods; we cannot tell our course by the stars, nor the hour of the day by the sun. It is well if we can swim and skate. We are afraid of a horse, of a cow, of a dog, of a snake, of a spider. The Roman rule was to teach a boy nothing that he could not learn standing. The old English rule was, "All summer in the field, and all winter in the study." And it seems as if a man should learn to plant, or to fish, or to hunt, that he might secure his subsistence at all events and not be painful to his friends and fellowmen. The lessons of science should be experimental also. The sight of a planet through a telescope is worth all the course on astronomy; the shock of the electric spark in the elbow outvalues all the theories; the taste of the nitrous oxide, the firing of an artificial volcano, are better than volumes of chemistry.

— Reading No. 4 —

ROBERT OWEN: CALL FOR A WORLD CONVENTION, 1845 [4]

Like so many others active in the reform movements, Fanny Wright and George Henry Evans and John B. Gough, for example, Robert Owen came from Britain,

[4] From Robert Owen, "Address on Leaving the United States for Europe," June 1, 1845, in J. R. Commons, *et al., Documentary History of American Industrial Society* (Cleveland, 1910) VII, 174-5.

and represents well both the intimate interrelations of the British and American reform activities, and the role that the United States was assigned as a kind of experimental laboratory for reform. He represents, too, the limitless ambition of the more extreme reformers: not content with one problem at a time, they undertook nothing less than a moral regeneration of mankind.

✔   ✔   ✔

All great improvements commence with one or a few, and these, by judicious measures, interest more and more, until a sufficient number unite to accomplish the object. There is an admirable spirit abroad anxiously looking out for the right commencement of this change and bold truths announced in the pure spirit of charity will now accomplish that object. Let then the proper measures to create this public opinion be now adopted, and let all good men of every class, sect, party and state unite for this Godlike purpose.

To this end let a Convention be called of delegates from every State and territory in the Union, to consider what practical measures can be immediately carried into execution to apply the enormous means to secure prosperity for all the people of these States, that they may become an example to the world of what, with sound judgment, in peace, with order and with the least injury and the most benefit to every one, from the highest to the lowest, may be done.

But what is every one's business is no one's in particular, and is too often neglected by all. I, therefore, feeling a deep interest in the immediate improvement of our race, recommend such Convention to be called the "World's Convention," to consider what measures of a practical character can be adopted to ensure the immediate benefit of every class, without violence, contest or competition, and especially what can be done to well educate and employ the uneducated and unemployed, to fit them for the superior state of society, to create which, for all the means are now so superabundant, not only in these States, but wherever men need to live; or it may be called "The World's Convention" to emancipate the human race from ignorance, poverty, division, sin and misery.

The chief business of my life has been, so far, to prepare all classes, from the highest to the lowest, for this great change in the condition of humanity in this world, and thus, in the best manner to prepare it for all future changes, whatever they may be, after we shall have done all in our power to ensure knowledge, goodness and happiness in our present mode of existence.

— Reading No. 5 —

HORACE GREELEY: REFORMS AND REFORMERS [5]

Horace Greeley was not only the greatest and most influential editor of his day, but the nearest thing to a Universal Reformer to be found in New York; appropriately enough, like those other leading New York reformers, W. C. Bryant and the Tappan brothers, he came out of New England. He had, perhaps, a wider acquaintance with reformers than any other American of his day, for his interests were political and economic as well as moral and intellectual, western as well as eastern. Late in life he wrote a fascinating volume of Recollections; it is from this that we draw this brief interpretation of the Reformer.

✓   ✓   ✓

The true Reformer turns his eyes first inward, scrutinizing himself, his habits, purposes, efforts, enjoyments, asking, What signifies this? and this? and wherein is its justification? This daily provision of meat and drink,—is its end nourishment and its incident enjoyment? or are the poles reversed, and do I eat and drink for the grati-

[5] Horace Greeley, "Reforms and Reformers," in *Recollections of a Busy Life* (New York, 1868), 502-3, 507-9.

fication of appetite, hoping, or trusting, or blindly guess-
ing, that, since it satiatès my desires, it must satisfy also
my needs? Is it requisite that all the zones and continents
should be ransacked to build up the fleeting earthly
tabernacle of this immortal spirit? Is not the soul rather
submerged, stifled, drowned, in this incessant idolizing,
feasting, pampering of the body? These sumptuous enter-
tainments, wherein the palate has everything, the soul
nothing,—what faculty, whether of body or mind, do
they brighten or strengthen? Why should a score of animals render up their lives to furnish forth my day's dinner, if my own life is thereby rendered neither surer nor
nobler? Why gorge myself with dainties which cloud the
brain and clog the step, if the common grains and fruits
and roots and water afford precisely the same sustenance
in simpler and less cloying guise, and are far more con-
ducive to health, strength, elasticity, longevity? Can a
man worthily surrender his life to the mere acquiring
and absorbing of food, thus alternating only from the
state of a beast of burden to that of a beast of prey?
Above all, why should I fire my blood and sear my brain
with liquors which give a temporary exhilaration to the
spirits at the cost of permanent depravation and disorder
to the whole physical frame? In short, why should I live
for and in my appetites, if these were Divinely created
to serve and sustain, not master and dethrone, the spirit
to which this earthly frame is but a husk, a tent, a halt-
ing-place, in an exalted, deathless career? If the life be
indeed more than meat, why shall not the meat recognize
and attest that fact? And thus the sincere Reformer, in
the very outset of his course, becomes a "tee-total"
fanatic, represented by the knavish and regarded by the
vulgar as a foe to all enjoyment and cheer, insisting that
mankind shall conform to his crotchets, and live on bran-
bread and blue cold water.

Turning his eyes away from himself, he scans the relations of man with man, under which labor is performed
and service secured, and finds, not absolute Justice, much
less Love, but Necessity on the one hand, Advantage on
the other, presiding over the general interchange of good
offices among mankind. In the market, on the exchange,
we meet no recognition of the brotherhood of the human

race. A famine in one country is a godsend to the grain-growers and flour-speculators of another. An excess of immigration enhances the cost of food while depressing the wages of labor, adding in both ways to the wealth of the forehanded, who find their only drawback to the increased burdens of pauperism. Thus the mansion and the hovel rise side by side, and where sheriffs are abundant is hanging most frequent. One man's necessity being another's opportunity, we have no right to be surprised or indignant that the general system colminates, by an inexorably logical process, in the existence and stubborn maintenance of Human Slavery. . . .

The great, the all-embracing Reform of our age is therefore the SOCIAL Reform,—that which seeks to lift the Laboring Class, as such,—not out of labor, by any means,—but out of ignorance, inefficiency, dependence, and want, and place them in a position of partnership and recognized mutual helpfulness with the suppliers of the Capital which they render fruitful and efficient. It is easily said that this is the case now; but, practically, the fact is otherwise. The man who has only labor to barter for wages or bread looks up to the buyer of his sole commodity as a benefactor; the master and journeyman, farmer and hired man, lender and borrower, mistress and servant, do *not* stand on a recognized footing of reciprocal benefaction. True, self-interest is the acknowledged impulse of either party; the lender, the employer, parts with his money only to increase it, and so, it would seem, is entitled to prompt payment or faithful service,—not, specially, to gratitude. He who pays a bushel of fair wheat for a day's work at sowing for next year's harvest has simply exchanged a modicum of his property for other property, to him of greater value; and so has no sort of claim to an unreciprocated obeisance from the other party to the bargain. But so long as there shall be ten who would gladly borrow to one disposed and able to lend, and many more anxious to be hired than others able and willing to employ them, there always will be a natural eagerness of competition for loans, advances, employment, and a resulting deference of borrower to lender, employed to employer. He who may hire or not, as to him shall seem profitable, is independent; while he who must be hired or starve exists at others' mercy. Not till

Society shall be so adjusted, so organized, that whoever is willing to work shall assuredly *have* work, and fair recompense for doing it, as readily as he who has gold may exchange it for more portable notes, will the laborer be placed on a footing of justice and rightful independence. He who is able and willing to give work for bread is not essentially a pauper; he does not desire to abstract without recompense from the aggregate of the world's goods and chattels; he is not rightfully a beggar. Wishing only to convert his own muscular energy into bread, it is not merely his but every man's interest that the opportunity should be afforded him,—nay, it is the clear *duty* of Society to render such exchange at all times practicable and convenient.

— Reading No. 6 —

THEODORE PARKER: A BRIEF HISTORY OF NEW ENGLAND REFORM [6]

Theodore Parker, known in his day as The Great American Preacher, was the very epitome of the New England reformer. As with Channing, Emerson, Ripley, and so many others, he came out of Harvard, and out of the Unitarian Church, and as with them his approach to reform was spiritual and moral. Parker himself left no aspect of reform untouched: religion, education, labor, woman's rights, war, and above all slavery. A man of volcanic energies, he contributed as much through his pen as with his voice. At the end of his life he reviewed

[6] From Theodore Parker, "Theodore Parker's Experience as a Minister," in Frances Cobbe, *Collected Works of Theodore Parker* (London, 1865) XII, 277-82.

his experiences as a minister; it is from this moving document that we have taken this brief account of the ferment of reform in the New England of the 'forties and 'fifties.

✓   ✓   ✓

Mr Garrison, with his friends, inheriting what was best in the Puritan founders of New England, fired with the zeal of the Hebrew prophets and Christian martyrs, while they were animated with a spirit of humanity rarely found in any of the three, was beginning his noble work, but in a style so humble that, after much search, the police of Boston discovered there was nothing dangerous in it, for "his only visible auxiliary was a negro boy." Dr Channing was in the full maturity of his powers, and after long preaching the dignity of man as an abstraction, and piety as a purely inward life, with rare and winsome eloquence, and ever progressive humanity, began to apply his sublime doctrines to actual life in the individual, the state, and the church. In the name of Christianity, the great American Unitarian called for the reform of the drunkard, the elevation of the poor, the instruction of the ignorant, and, above all, for the liberation of the American slave. A remarkable man, his instinct of progress grew stronger the more he travelled and the further he went, for he surrounded himself with young life. Horace Mann, with his coadjutors, began a great movement, to improve the public education of the people. Pierpont, single-handed, was fighting a grand and two-fold battle —against drunkenness in the street, and for righteousness in the pulpit—against fearful ecclesiastic odds, maintaining a minister's right and duty to oppose actual wickedness, however popular and destructive. The brilliant genius of Emerson rose in the winter nights, and hung over Boston, drawing the eyes of ingenuous young people to look up to that great, new star, a beauty and a mystery, which charmed for the moment, while it gave also perennial inspiration, as it led them forward along new paths, and toward new hopes. America had seen no such sight before; it is not less a blessed wonder now.

Besides, the Phrenologists, so ably represented by Spurzheim and Combe, were weakening the power of the old supernaturalism, leading men to study the constitution of man more wisely than before, and laying the

foundation on which many a beneficent structure was
soon to rise. The writings of Wordsworth were becoming
familiar to the thoughtful lovers of nature and of man,
and drawing men to natural piety. Carlyle's works got
reprinted at Boston, diffusing a strong, and then, also, a
healthy influence on old and young. The writings of
Coleridge were reprinted in America, all of them "aids
to reflection," and brilliant with the scattered sparks of
genius; they incited many to think, more especially young
Trinitarian ministers; and, spite of the lack of both his-
toric and philosophic accuracy, and the utter absence of
all proportion in his writings; spite of his haste, his vanity,
prejudice, sophistry, confusion, and opium—he yet did
great service in New-England, helping to emancipate en-
thralled minds. The works of Cousin, more systematic,
and more profound as a whole, and far more catholic
and comprehensive, continental, not insular, in his range,
also became familiar to the Americans—reviews and
translations going where the eloquent original was not
heard—and helped to free the young mind from the gross
sensationalism of the academic philosophy on one side,
and the grosser supernaturalism of the ecclesiastic theology on the other.

The German language, hitherto the priceless treasure
of a few, was becoming well known, and many were
thereby made acquainted with the most original, deep,
bold, comprehensive, and wealthy literature in the world,
full of theologic and philosophic thought. Thus, a great
storehouse was opened to such as were earnestly in quest
of truth. Young Mr Strauss, in whom genius for criticism was united with extraordinary learning and rare
facility of philosophic speech, wrote his "Life of Jesus,"
where he rigidly scrutinized the genuineness of the Gos-
pels and the authenticity of their contents, and, with
scientific calmness, brought every statement to his steady
scales, weighing it, not always justly, as I think, but im-
partially always, with philosophic coolness and delibera-
tion. The most formidable assailant of the ecclesiastical
theology of Christendom, he roused a host of foes, whose
writings—mainly ill-tempered, insolent, and sophistical—
it was very profitable for a young man to read.

The value of Christian miracles, not the question of
fact, was discussed at Boston, as never before in America.

Prophecy had been thought the Jachin, and miracles the Boaz, whereon alone Christianity could rest; but, said some, if both be shaken down, the Lord's house will not fall. The claims of ecclesiastical tradition came up to be settled anew; and young men, walking solitary through the moonlight, asked, "Which is to be permanent master —a single accident in human history, nay, perchance only the whim of some anonymous dreamer, or the substance of human nature, greatening with continual development, and

Not without access of unexpected strength?"

The question was also its answer.

The rights of labour were discussed with deep philanthropic feeling, and sometimes with profound thought, metaphysic and economic both. The works of Charles Fourier—a strange, fantastic, visionary man, no doubt, but gifted also with amazing insight of the truths of social science—shed some light in these dark places of speculation. Mr Ripley, a born Democrat, in the high sense of that abused word, and one of the best cultured and most enlightened men in America, made an attempt at Brookfarm in West Roxbury, so to organize society that the results of labour should remain in the workman's hand, and not slip thence to the trader's till; that there should be "no exploitation of man by man," but toil and thought, hard work and high culture, should be united in the same person.

The natural rights of women began to be inquired into, and publicly discussed; while in private, great pains were taken in the chief towns of New-England, to furnish a thorough and comprehensive education to such young maidens as were born with two talents, mind and money.

Of course, a strong reaction followed. . . .

This reaction was supported by the ministers in the great churches of commerce, and by the old literary periodicals, which never knew a star was risen till men wondered at it in the zenith; the Unitarian journals gradually went over to the opponents of freedom and progress, with lofty scorn rejecting their former principles, and repeating the conduct they had once complained of; Cambridge and Princeton seemed to be interchanging cards. From such hands Cousin and Emerson could not receive needed criticism, but only vulgar abuse. Dr Channing could "not draw a long breath in Boston," where he found the successors of Paul trembling before the successors of Felix. Even Trinitarian Moses Stuart seemed scarcely safe in his hard-bottomed Hopkinsian chair, at Andover. The Trinitarian ministers and city schoolmasters galled Horace Mann with continual assaults on his measures for educating the people. Unitarian ministers struck hands with wealthy liquor dealers to drive Mr Pierpoint from his pulpit, where he valiantly preached "temperance, righteousness, and judgment to come," appealing to "a day after to-day." Prominent anti-slavery men were dropped out of all wealthy society in Boston, their former friends not knowing them in the streets; Mr. Garrison was mobbed by men in handsome coats, and found defence from their fury only in a jail; an assembly of women, consulting for the liberation of their darker sisters, was driven with hootings into the street. The Attorney-General of Massachusetts brought an indictment for blasphemy against a country minister, one of the most learned Biblical scholars in America, for publicly proving that none of the "Messianic prophecies" of the Old Testament was ever fulfilled by Jesus of Nazareth, who accordingly was not the expected Christ of the Jews. Abner Kneeland, editor of a newspaper, in which he boasted of the name "Infidel," was clapped in jail for writing against the ecclesiastical notion of God, the last man ever punished for blasphemy in the State. At the beck of a Virginian slave-holder, the Governor of Massachusetts suggested to the legislature the expediency of abridging the old New-England liberty of speech.

The movement party established a new quarterly, the *Dial,* wherein their wisdom and their folly rode together on the same saddle, to the amazement of lookers-on. The short-lived journal had a narrow circulation, but its most significant papers were scattered wide by newspapers which copied them. A *Quarterly Review* was also established by Mr Brownson, then a Unitarian minister and "sceptical democrat" of the most extravagant class, but now a Catholic, a powerful advocate of material and spiritual despotism, and perhaps the ablest writer in America against the rights of man and the welfare of his race. In this he diffused important philosophic ideas,

displayed and disciplined his own extraordinary talents
for philosophic thought and popular writings, and directed
them towards Democracy, Transcendentalism, "New
Views," and the "Progress of the Species."

I count it a piece of good fortune that I was a young
man when these things were taking place, when great
questions were discussed, and the public had not yet
taken sides.

II

UTOPIANISM

— Reading No. 7 —

FRANCES WRIGHT: REFORM, RADICAL AND UNIVERSAL, 1829[7]

*Utopianism was one expression of the reform senti-
ment of the day, and the American landscape was lit-
tered with straggling Utopias. There was nothing new
about Utopianism—after all, America itself had long
been the Utopia of European dreamers and intellectuals;
what was new was the effort to escape from America
itself, and from all of the problems and the potentialities*

[7] From Frances Wright, *A Course of Popular Lectures* (New
York, 1829) Lecture VII, "Of Existing Evils and Their
Remedy."

*of American society. Certainly it was easier to establish
a Utopia on the American frontier than elsewhere: there
was land enough; there was a habit of voluntary association; there was freedom for experimentation. Many
of the American Utopias were inspired from abroad—
notably those patterned on the ideas of Charles Fourier;
others, like Robert Owen's New Harmony or Frances
Wright's Nashoba, were organized by idealists from over-
seas. Frances Wright, a Scotswoman of fortune who had
toured America with Lafayette in 1824, spent part of her
fortune on Nashoba, an ill-fated emancipation-commu-
nity in Tennessee; she joined Robert Dale Owen in edit-
ing the* New Harmony Gazette; *then helped organize, and
lead, the short-lived Workingmen's Party in New York.
She was a Universal Reformer, and an indefatigable
writer; this call for Universal Reform appeared in an
early book based on a series of lectures. We add a few
lines from Bryant's "Ode to Miss Wright," written the
year of publication of these essays.*

✓   ✓   ✓

Who speaks of liberty while the human mind is in
chains? Who of equality while the thousands are in
squalid wretchedness, the millions harassed with health-
destroying labour, the few afflicted with health-destroying
idleness, and all tormented by health-destroying solici-
tude? Look abroad on the misery which is gaining on the
land! Mark the strife, and the discord, and the jealousies,
the shock of interests and opinions, the hatreds of sect,
the estrangements of class, the pride of wealth, the de-
basement of poverty, the helplessness of youth unprotected, of age uncomforted, of industry unrewarded, of
ignorance unenlightened, of vice unreclaimed, of misery
unpitied, of sickness, hunger, and nakedness unsatisfied,
unalleviated, and unheeded. Go! mark all the wrongs and
the wretchedness with which the eye and the ear and
the heart are familiar, and then echo in triumph and
celebrate in jubilee the insulting declaration—*all men are
free and equal!*

That evils exist, none that have eyes, ears, and hearts
can dispute. That these evils are on the increase, none
who have watched the fluctuations of trade, the sinking
price of labour, the growth of pauperism, and the increase

of crime, will dispute. Little need be said here to the people of Philadelphia. The researches made by the public spirited among their own citizens, have but too well substantiated the suffering condition of a large mass of their population. In Boston, in New-York, in Baltimore, the voice of distress hath, in like manner, burst the barriers raised, and so long sustained, by the pride of honest industry, unused to ask from charity what it hath been wont to earn by the sweat of the brow. In each and every city necessity has constrained inquiry; and in each and every city inquiry has elicited the same appalling facts: that the hardest labour is often without a reward adequate to the sustenance of the labourer; that when, by over exertion and all the diseases, and often vices, which excess of exertion induces, the labourer, whose patient sedulous industry supplies the community with all its comforts, and the rich with all their luxuries—when he, I say, is brought to an untimely grave by those exertions which, while sustaining the life of others, cut short his own—when he is mowed down by that labour whose products form the boasted wealth of the state, he leaves a family, to whom the strength of his manhood had barely furnished bread, to lean upon the weakness of a soul-stricken mother, and hurry her to the grave of her father. . . .

Reform, and that not slight nor partial, but radical and universal, is called for. All must admit that no such reform—that is, that no remedy commensurate with the evil, has been suggested, and would we but reflect, we should perceive that no efficient remedy *can* be suggested or, if suggested, applied, until the people are generally engaged in its discovery and its application for themselves. . . .

As our time is short . . . I must hasten to the rapid development of the system of instruction and protection, which has occurred to me as capable, and alone capable, of opening the door to universal reform.

In lieu of all common schools, high schools, colleges, seminaries, houses of refuge, or any other juvenile institution, instructional or protective, I would suggest that the state legislatures be directed (after laying off the whole in townships or hundreds) to organize, at suitable distances, and in convenient and healthy situations, es-

tablishments for the general reception of all the children
resident within the said school district. These establishments to be devoted, severally, to children between a certain age. Say, the first, infants between two and four, or
two and six, according to the density of the population,
and such other local circumstances as might render a
greater or less number of establishments necessary or
practicable. The next to receive children from four to
eight, or six to twelve years. The next from twelve to
sixteen, or to an older age if found desirable. Each establishment to be furnished with instructors in every branch
of knowledge, intellectual and operative, with all the apparatus, land, and conveniences necessary for the best
development of all knowledge; the same, whether operative or intellectual, being always calculated to the age
and strength of the pupils.

To obviate, in the commencement, every evil result
possible from the first mixture of a young population,
so variously raised in error or neglect, a due separation
should be made in each establishment; by which means
those entering with bad habits would be kept apart from
the others until corrected. How rapidly reform may be
effected on the plastic disposition of childhood, has been
sufficiently proved in your houses of refuge, more especially when such establishments have been under *liberal*
superintendence, as was formerly the case in New-York.
Under their orthodox directors, those asylums of youth
have been converted into jails.

It will be understood that, in the proposed establishments, the children would pass from one to the other in
regular succession, and that the parents who would necessarily be resident in their close neighbourhood, could
visit the children at suitable hours, but, in no case, in-
terfere with or interrupt the rules of the institution.

In the older establishments, the well directed and well
protected labour of the pupil would, in time, suffice for,
and then exceed their own support; when the surplus
might be devoted to the maintenance of the infant establishments.

In the beginning, and until all debt was cleared off,
and so long as the same should be found favourable to
the promotion of these best palladiums of a nation's hap-

piness, a double tax might be at once expedient and
politic. . . .

In these nurseries of a free nation, no inequality must
be allowed to enter. Fed at a common board; clothed in
a common garb, uniting neatness with simplicity and con-
venience; raised in the exercise of common duties, in the
acquirement of the same knowledge and practice of the
same industry, varied only according to individual tastes
and capabilities; in the exercise of the same virtues, in
the employment of the same pleasures; in the study of
the same nature; in pursuit of the same object—their own
and each other's happiness—say! would not such a race,
when arrived at manhood and womanhood, work out
the reform of society—perfect the free institutions of
America.

ODE TO MISS WRIGHT

Thou wonder of the age, from whom
Religion waits her final doom,
Her quiet death, her euthanasia,
Thou in whose eloquence and bloom
The age beholds a new Aspasia!

WILLIAM CULLEN BRYANT, 1829

— Reading No. 8 —

BRONSON ALCOTT'S FRUITLANDS, 1843[8]

*Bronson Alcott, already famous for his educational
experiments* (see Reading No. 42) *projected his private*

[8] From Clara Endicott Sears, comp. "Bronson Alcott's Fruitlands, . . ." (Boston, Houghton, Mifflin Co., 1915) 50-52.

*Utopian Community after a visit to England in 1842; it
was perhaps the most austere of the various Utopian enterprises, and the most impracticable. Though it lasted
only seven months it gave us not only one of the more
characteristic chapters in the history of American Utopianism but—in Louisa May Alcott's delightful "Trans-
cendental Wild Oats"—one of the entertaining chapters
in American literature.*

✦   ✦   ✦

We rise with early dawn, begin the day with cold
bathing, succeeded by a music lesson, and then a chaste
repast. Each one finds occupation until the meridian meal,
when usually some interesting and deep-searching conversation gives rest to the body and development to the
mind. Occupation, according to the season and the
weather, engages us out of doors or within, until the
evening meal,—when we again assemble in social com-
munion, prolonged generally until sunset, when we resort to sweet repose for the next day's activity.

In these steps of reform we do not rely as much on
scientific reasoning or physiological skill, as on the Spirit's
dictates. The pure soul, by the law of its own nature,
adopts a pure diet and cleanly customs; nor needs detailed instruction for daily conduct. On a revision of our
proceedings it would seem, that if we were in the right
course in our particular instance, the greater part of
man's duty consists in leaving alone much that he is in
the habit of doing. It is a fasting from the present activity,
rather than an increased indulgence in it, which, with
patient watchfulness tends to newness of life. "Shall I
sip tea or coffee?" the inquiry may be. No; abstain from
all ardent, as from alcoholic drinks. "Shall I consume
pork, beef, or mutton?" Not if you value health or life.
"Shall I stimulate with milk?" No. "Shall I warm my
bathing water?" Not if cheerfulness is valuable. "Shall I
clothe in many garments?" Not if purity is aimed at.
"Shall I prolong my dark hours, consuming animal oil
and losing bright daylight in the morning?" Not if a
clear mind is an object. "Shall I teach my children the
dogmas inflicted on myself, under the pretence that I am
transmitting truth?" Nay, if you love them intrude not
these between them and the Spirit of all Truth. "Shall

I subjugate cattle?" "Shall I trade?" "Shall I claim property in any created thing?" "Shall I interest myself in politics?" To how many of these questions could we ask them deeply enough, could they be heard as having relation to our eternal welfare, would the response be "Abstain"? Be not so active to do, as sincere to be. Being in preference to doing, is the great aim and this comes to us rather by a resigned willingness than a wilful activity;—which is indeed a check to all divine growth. Outward abstinence is a sign of inward fulness; and the only source of true progress is inward. We may occupy ourselves actively in human improvements;—but these unless inwardly well-impelled, never attain to, but rather hinder, divine progress in man. During the utterance of this narrative it has undergone a change in its personal expression which might offend the hypercritical; but we feel assured that you will kindly accept it as unartful offering of both your friends in ceaseless aspiration.

CHARLES LANE,
A. BRONSON ALCOTT.

Harvard, Mass.,
   August, 1843.

— Reading No. 9 —

ELIZABETH PEABODY: ACCOUNT OF BROOK FARM[9]

Though by no means the largest, the most important, or the most characteristic Utopian community, Brook Farm was undoubtedly the most famous. Its fame came in part from the distinction of its members—Ripley, Hawthorne, Charles A. Dana, Margaret Fuller, John S.

[9] From Elizabeth Peabody, *Brook Farm,* reprinted in John H. Noyes, *History of American Socialisms* (Philadelphia, 1870) 114-117.

Dwight and others—and from the literature which it inspired, notably Hawthorne's Blithedale Romance. *Established at West Roxbury, Massachusetts, in 1841, it flourished, or at least endured, until a disastrous fire brought it to an end in 1846. Not until 1845 did it become a Fourieristic Phalanx. Elizabeth Peabody—one of the famous Peabody sisters—was not a member, but much of the preliminary planning of Brook Farm went on in her famous bookshop, and most of those who participated in the experiment were friends or acquaintances.*

✓   ✓   ✓

In order to live a religious and moral life worthy the name, they feel it is necessary to come out in some degree from the world, and to form themselves into a community of property, so far as to exclude competition and the ordinary rules of trade; while they reserve sufficient private property, or the means of obtaining it, for all purposes of independence, and isolation at will. They have bought a farm, in order to make agriculture the basis of their life, it being the most direct and simple in relation to nature. A true life, although it aims beyond the highest star, is redolent of the healthy earth. The perfume of clover lingers about it. The lowing of cattle is the natural bass to the melody of human voices. . . .

The plan of the Community, as an economy, is in brief this: for all who have property to take stock, and receive a fixed interest thereon: then to keep house or board in commons, as they shall severally desire, at the cost of provisions purchased at wholesale, or raised on the farm; and for all to labor in community, and be paid at a certain rate an hour, choosing their own number of hours, and their own kind of work. With the results of this labor and their interest, they are to pay their board, and also purchase whatever else they require at cost, at the warehouses of the Community, which are to be filled by the Community as such. To perfect this economy, in the course of time they must have all trades and all modes of business carried on among themselves, from the lowest mechanical trade, which contributes to the health and comfort of life, to the finest art, which adorns it with food or drapery for the mind.

All labor, whether bodily or intellectual, is to be paid

at the same rate of wages; on the principle that as the labor becomes merely bodily, it is a greater sacrifice to the individual laborer to give his time to it; because time is desirable for the cultivation of the intellectual, in exact proportion to ignorance. Besides, intellectual labor involves in itself higher pleasures, and is more its own reward, than bodily labor. * * *

After becoming members of this Community, none will be engaged merely in bodily labor. The hours of labor for the Association will be limited by a general law, and can be curtailed at the will of the individual still more; and means will be given to all for intellectual improvement and for social intercourse, calculated to refine and expand. The hours redeemed from labor by community, will not be re-applied to the acquisition of wealth, but to the production of intellectual goods. This Community aims to be rich, not in the metallic representative of wealth, but in the wealth itself, which money should represent; namely, LEISURE TO LIVE IN ALL THE FACULTIES OF THE SOUL. As a Community, it will traffic with the world at large, in the products of agricultural labor; and it will sell education to as many young persons as can be domesticated in the families, and enter into the common life with their own children. In the end it hopes to be enabled to provide, not only all the necessaries, but all the elegances desirable for bodily and for spiritual health: books, apparatus, collections for science, works of art, means of beautiful amusement. These things are to be common to all; and thus that object, which alone gilds and refines the passion for individual accumulation, will no longer exist for desire, and whenever the sordid passion appears, it will be seen in its naked selfishness. In its ultimate success, the Community will realize all the ends which selfishness seeks, but involved in spiritual blessings, which only greatness of soul can aspire after.

And the requisitions on the individuals, it is believed, will make this the order forever. The spiritual good will always be the condition of the temporal. Every one must labor for the Community in a reasonable degree, or not taste its benefits. * * * Whoever is willing to receive from his fellow men that for which he gives no equivalent, will stay away from its precincts forever. But who-

ever shall surrender himself to its principles, shall find
that its yoke is easy and its burden light. Everything can
be said of it, in a degree, which Christ said of his kingdom, and therefore it is believed that in some measure
it does embody his idea. For its gate of entrance is strait
and narrow. It is literally a pearl hidden in a field. Those
only who are willing to lose their life for its sake shall
find it. Its voice is that which sent the young man sor-
rowing away: 'Go sell all thy goods and give to the poor,
and then come and follow me.' 'Seek first the kingdom
of Heaven and its righteousness, and all other things
shall be added to you.' * * *

There may be some persons at a distance, who will
ask, To what degree has this Community gone into operation? We can not answer this with precision, but we
have a right to say that it has purchased the farm which
some of its members cultivated for a year with success,
by way of trying their love and skill for agricultural
labor; that in the only house they are as yet rich
enough to own, is collected a large family, including
several boarding scholars, and that all work and study
together. They seem to be glad to know of all who
desire to join them in the spirit, that at any moment,
when they are able to enlarge their habitations, they may
call together those that belong to them.

— Reading No. 10 —

ADIN BALLOU EXPLAINS THE HOPEDALE COMMUNITY [10]

*The Hopedale Community was founded at Milford,
Massachusetts, the same year as Brook Farm; its purpose was more explicitly moral and religious—"to be*

[10] From Adin Ballou, *History of the Hopedale Community*
(Lowell, 1897) 10-13.

*an experiment in the science of a divine order of society,
or an attempt to actualize in organic form the kingdom
of God on earth." Its founder, and for many years its
leader, was Adin Ballou, member of a remarkable family
of Universalist clergymen. The Community lasted well
into the 1850's, when it was transformed into a highly
successful manufacturing community.*

In several fundamental particulars were we openly and
uncompromisingly arrayed against the prevailing theory
and practice of the world at large about us.

(1) The great overshadowing *War System,* everywhere
deemed essential to the maintenance of public order and
the security of the common welfare, with its multiplex
enginery of destruction, its appalling record of devasta-
tion, bloodshed, and death; its awful burden of degradation, poverty, and wretchedness, crushing the life out of
vast multitudes of people; its manifold barbarities and
cruelties, subversive of the essential principles and vital
spirit of the Gospel of Christ, we unqualifiedly condemned and repudiated.

(2) The vast complex mechanism of *Politico-civil Government* in its existing form and mode of administration,
based upon injurious and death-dealing force as a final
resort, and claiming the unquestioning allegiance and support of its subjects, with its ubiquitous agencies, offices,
emoluments, excitements, honors, and rewards, its subtle
methods of control and usurpations of authority, its disregard of the requirements of the moral law and of the
rights of the weak and defenceless, the chicanery and
corruption that often enter into its management, shaping
its policy and dictating its legislation—all this was tran-
scended and set aside by us in our declared loyalty to
that kingdom which is "not of this world," "whose
officers are peace and its exactors righteousness," and
wherein those that are chief and would be accounted
greatest are servants of all.

(3) The abounding *spirit of competition, rivalry, self-
aggrandizement, and open antagonism* which dominates
industry and trade, whereby mammon worship is per-
petually encouraged and mutual helpfulness ignored;
whereby the strong make victims of the weak, the cunning

and unscrupulous outwit and overreach the honest, simple-minded, and self-respecting, the arrogant and heartless take advantage of the necessities of the poor and un-fortunate, resulting in class distinctions, in gross in-equalities of condition, in revolting extremes of wealth and poverty, of prodigal luxury and famishing want, of gorgeous display and loathesome destitution, engender-ing discontent, ill-will, resentment, animosity, hatred, and sometimes the spirit of revenge and open violence;—all this, and especially the state of things producing it, we condemned and repudiated as utterly opposed to our doctrine of human brotherhood, . . .

Another consideration of no trifling importance came in as a factor of the problem whose solution was command-ing our attention, and no doubt had considerable influence in determining our future course. Our acknowledged "Standard" comtemplated and required on our part, not only a devotion to whatever might conduce in a general way and by the more quiet methods of moral enlighten-ment and spiritual regeneration and growth to the prog-ress and redemption of mankind, but also a deep and active interest in those specific reforms which were then agitating the public mind and pressing their claims home upon the hearts and consciences of all those who loved God and their fellowmen. Recognizing and accepting the obligations imposed upon us in that respect, we had heartily espoused the Anti-Slavery, Temperance, and Peace movements, and had borne faithful witness in the pulpit and elsewhere against the great evils they were designed to overcome and banish from the world.

— Reading No. 11 —

REPORT OF THE TRUMBULL PHALANX, 1846[11]

[11] From *The Harbinger,* 20 February 1847, in Commons, *et al., Documentary History of American Industrial Society,* VII, 247 ff.

*Horace Greeley, Parke Godwin, and Albert Brisbane
—all working and writing in New York City—early
came under the influence of the doctrines of Charles
Fourier, the French socialist who as early as 1808 had
advanced a theory of cooperative communism, organized
in "associations" or "phalanxes." In 1843 Brisbane wrote*
A Concise Exposition of the Doctrine of Association, *and
the next year Parke Godwin followed with* A Popular
View of the Doctrines of Fourier. *These publications, and
Horace Greeley's enthusiastic editorials and essays, inspired the formation of over forty Fourieristic phalanxes
in the next decade or so. No fewer than eight of these
were founded in Ohio. We give here a report of one of
the Ohio phalanxes, the Trumbull, of Braceville, Ohio,
and call attention particularly to the final observation:
"We have nothing to fear . . . but our own unfaithfulness."*

✓   ✓   ✓

TRUMBULL PHALANX

We are happy to present the following "Report of
the Productions and Improvements of the Trumbull
Phalanx for 1846," which we have received from the
Secretary of that Association. It will be perceived that
our friends bear their testimony to the pleasure and
advantage of the Associative life, even in the rude and
imperfect forms which are all that at present can be
realized. We have never pretended that the little at-
tempts at Association, now in progress, are able to il-
lustrate the character and effects of the Combined Order: they are little more than spontaneous gatherings of
friends, inspired with a sincere zeal for an improved
order of society, full of faith in God, in Humanity, and
in the Future, but generally without adequate science,
without capital, without the material facilities, which
are essential to a complete realization of a true Social
Order. But in the humblest degree of Associated life
of which we have had any experience, there is an interest, a charm, a consciousness of approaching at least,
the true way, which cannot be felt in the proudest
abodes of Civilization. The moral tone, the sincere, ele-
vated affections, the freedom from the clutch-all system,
which prevails in common society, bind the heart to

life in Association; and hence we rejoice in all the evidence of prosperity which we receive from time to time, in the infant Associations that are now struggling for existence, while we wait in hope for the day when a Model Phalanx shall combine the strength of friends that is now scattered, and exhibit to the world a splendid demonstration of the truth of our principles.

It is proper to state that having tried the combined Household system, or General Boarding House, we have abandoned it entirely, and retreated to the separate Household. This we are forced to do for want of sufficient means to give variety and attraction to the common table, and there is now universal satisfaction with the present arrangement. Without doubt the time will come when the Combined system will be found preferable in economy, ease and attraction; but we have been taught by dear experience, that without sufficient wealth, edifices, machinery and knowledge of such establishments, it were far, far better not to attempt anything of the kind, but to take every thing in its own order, the simple and easy first, and not endeavor to secure what can only be the result of years. A Boarding House, however, is continued by a suitable family for the accommodation of the young men. It was found, last year, to have cost forty-seven cents per week, for men, for women and children less.

The above report for the year gives an idea of what we have been doing, and what materials we are accumulating for our future operations, and we can but say in addition that we are harmoniously united, living plain, common-sense lives, and are persuaded that our continued prosperity, that is, on the whole, is a cheering indication that we have nothing to fear in the future but our own unfaithfulness. N. C. MEEKER, Cor. Sec'y. Trumbull Phalanx, Braceville, Ohio, Dec. 26, 1846.

— Reading No. 12 —

JOHN H. NOYES: CONSTITUTION OF THE ONEIDA COMMUNITY, 1848 [12]

Certainly the most notorious, and probably the most successful, of the many Utopian communities was that established by John Humphrey Noyes on Oneida Creek in the burnt-over region of up-state New York. Noyes, a graduate of Dartmouth College and of Yale, had originally set up a Perfectionist community in Putney, Vermont; local hostility to his "complex marriage" system forced him, in 1848, to move to New York. By 1851 his Oneida community boasted over 200 members. Economically and socially it was highly successful, and flourished for over a quarter of a century. We give here Noyes' own statement of the institution, or practice, of "complex marriage."

✓   ✓   ✓

CHAPTER II.—*Showing that Marriage is not an institution of the Kingdom of Heaven, and must give place to Communism.*

PROPOSITION 5.—In the Kingdom of Heaven, the institution of marriage, which assigns the exclusive possession of one woman to one man, does not exist. Matt. 22: 23—30.

6.—In the Kingdom of Heaven the intimate union of life and interest, which in the world is limited to pairs, extends through the whole body of believers; i. e. complex marriage takes the place of simple. John 17: 21. . . .

[12] From John Humphrey Noyes, *History of American Socialisms* (Philadelphia, 1870) 624-31.

8.—Admitting that the Community principle of the day of Pentecost, in its actual operation at that time, extended only to material goods, yet we affirm that there is no intrinsic difference between property in persons and property in things; and that the same spirit which abolished exclusiveness in regard to money, would abolish, if circumstances allowed full scope to it, exclusiveness in regard to women and children. Paul expressly places property in women and property in goods in the same category, and speaks of them together, as ready to be abolished by the advent of the Kingdom of Heaven. "The time," says he, "is short; it remaineth that they that have wives be as though they had none; and they that buy as though they possessed not; for the fashion of this world passeth away." I Cor. 7: 29-31.

9.—The abolishment of appropriation is involved in the very nature of a true relation to Christ in the gospel. This we prove thus: The possessive feeling which expresses itself by the possessive pronoun *mine,* is the same in essence when it relate to persons, as when it relates to money or any other property. Amativeness and acquisitiveness are only different channels of one stream. They converge as we trace them to their source. . . .

10.—The abolishment of exclusiveness is involved in the love-relation required between all believers by the express injunction of Christ and the apostles, and by the whole tenor of the New Testament. "The new commandment is, that we love one another," and that, not by pairs, as in the world, but *en masse.* We are required to love one another fervently. The fashion of the world forbids a man and woman who are otherwise appropriated, to love one another fervently. But if they obey Christ they must do this; and whoever would allow them to do this, and yet would forbid them (on any other ground than that of present expediency), to express their unity, would "strain at a gnat and swallow a camel"; for unity of hearts is as much more important than any external expression of it, as a camel is larger than a gnat. . . .

13.—The law of marriage is the same in kind with the Jewish law concerning meats and drinks and holy days, of which Paul said that they were "contrary to us, and were taken out of the way, being nailed to the cross." Col. 2: 14. The plea in favor of the worldly social system, that it is not arbitrary, but founded in nature, will not bear investigation. All experience testifies (the theory of the novels to the contrary notwithstanding), that sexual love is not naturally restricted to pairs. Second marriages are contrary to the one-love theory, and yet are often the happiest marriages. Men and women find universally (however the fact may be concealed), that their susceptibility to love is not burnt out by one honey-moon, or satisfied by one lover. On the contrary, the secret history of the human heart will bear out the assertion that it is capable of loving any number of times and any number of persons, and that the more it loves the more it can love. This is the law of nature, thrust out of sight and condemned by common consent, and yet secretly known to all.

14.—The law of marriage "worketh wrath." 1. It provokes to secret adultery, actual or of the heart. 2. It ties together unmatched natures. 3. It sunders matched natures. 4. It gives to sexual appetite only a scanty and monotonous allowance, and so produces the natural vices of poverty, contraction of taste and stinginess or jealousy. 5. It makes no provision for the sexual appetite at the very time when that appetite is the strongest. By the custom of the world, marriage, in the average of cases, takes place at about the age of twenty-four; whereas puberty commences at the age of fourteen. For ten years, therefore, and that in the very flush of life, the sexual appetite is starved. This law of society bears hardest on females, because they have less opportunity of choosing their time of marriage than men. This discrepancy between the marriage system and nature, is one of the principal sources of the peculiar diseases of women, of prostitution, masturbation, and licentiousness in general.

III

POLITICAL REFORM

— Reading No. 13 —

GEORGE BANCROFT: THE PEOPLE IS ALWAYS FIRM AND SAGACIOUS, 1835[13]

Bancroft, the first major American historian, was also one of the first of the New England intellectuals to throw in his lot with the Jacksonian Democrats. It is sometimes forgotten that he was not only the author of a multi-volumed History of the United States, *but also Collector of the Port of Boston, Secretary of the Navy, and Minister to Great Britain and to Germany. He came as close to being the philosopher of Jacksonian democracy as any man of his generation; this statement of faith was first made as an oration at Williams College, in August 1835.*

✓   ✓   ✓

The best government rests on the people and not on the few, on persons and not on property, on the free development of public opinion and not on authority; because the munificent Author of our being has conferred the gifts

[13] From George Bancroft, *Office of the People in Art, Government and Religion, in Literary and Historical Miscellanies* (New York, 1855) 408 ff.

of mind upon every member of the human race without distinction of outward circumstances. Whatever of other possessions may be engrossed, mind asserts its own independence. Lands, estates, the produce of mines, the prolific abundance of the seas, may be usurped by a privileged class. Avarice, assuming the form of ambitious power, may grasp realm after realm, subdue continents, compass the earth in its schemes of aggrandizement, and sigh after other worlds; but mind eludes the power of appropriation; it exists only in its own individuality; it is a property which cannot be confiscated and cannot be torn away; it laughs at chains; it bursts from imprisonment; it defies monopoly. A government of equal rights must, therefore, rest upon mind; not wealth, not brute force, the sum of the moral intelligence of the community should rule the State. Prescription can no more assume to be a valid plea for political injustice; society studies to eradicate established abuses, and to bring social institutions and laws into harmony with moral right; not dismayed by the natural and necessary imperfections of all human effort, and not giving way to despair, because every hope does not at once ripen into fruit.

The public happiness is the true object of legislation, and can be secured only by the masses of mankind themselves awakening to the knowledge and the care of their own interests. Our free institutions have reversed the false and ignoble distinctions between men; and refusing to gratify the pride of caste, have acknowledged the common mind to be the true material for a commonwealth. Every thing has hitherto been done for the happy few. It is not possible to endow an aristocracy with greater benefits than they have already enjoyed; there is no room to hope that individuals will be more highly gifted or more fully developed than the greatest sages of past times. The world can advance only through the culture of the moral and intellectual powers of the people. To accomplish this end by means of the people themselves is the highest purpose of government. If it be the duty of the individual to strive after a perfection like the perfection of God, how much more ought a nation to be the image of Deity. The common mind is the true Parian marble, fit to be wrought into likeness to a God. The duty of America is to secure

the culture and the happiness of the masses by their
reliance on themselves.

The absence of the prejudices of the old world leaves us
here the opportunity of consulting independent truth; and
man is left to apply the instinct of freedom to every social
relation and public interest. We have approached so near
to nature, that we can hear her gentlest whispers; we have
made Humanity our lawgiver and our oracle; and, therefore, the nation receives, vivifies and applies principles,
which in Europe the wisest accept with distrust. Freedom
of mind and of conscience, freedom of the seas, freedom
of industry, equality of franchises, each great truth is
firmly grasped, comprehended and enforced; for the
multitude is neither rash nor fickle. In truth, it is less
fickle than those who profess to be its guides. Its natural
dialectics surpass the logic of the schools. Political action
has never been so consistent and so unwavering, as when
it results from a feeling or a principle, diffused through
society. The people is firm and tranquil in its movements,
and necessarily acts with moderation, because it becomes
but slowly impregnated with new ideas; and effects no
changes, except in harmony with the knowledge which it
has acquired. Besides, where it is permanently possessed
of power, there exists neither the occasion nor the desire
for frequent change. It is not the parent of tumult; sedition
is bred in the lap of luxury, and its chosen emissaries
are the beggared spendthrift and the impoverished libertine. The government by the people is in very truth the
strongest government in the world. Discarding the im-
plements of terror, it dares to rule by moral force, and has
its citadel in the heart.

Such is the political system which rests on reason, reflection, and the free expression of deliberate choice.
There may be those who scoff at the suggestion, that the
decision of the whole is to be preferred to the judgment of
the enlightened few. They say in their hearts that the
masses are ignorant; that farmers know nothing of legislation; that mechanics should not quit their workshops to
join in forming public opinion. But true political science
does indeed venerate the masses. It maintains, not as has
been perversely asserted, that "the people can make
right," but that the people can DISCERN right. Individuals
are but shadows, too often engrossed by the pursuit of

shadows; the race is immortal: individuals are of limited sagacity; the common mind is infinite in its experience: individuals are languid and blind; the many are ever wakeful: individuals are corrupt; the race has been redeemed: individuals are time-serving; the masses are fearless: individuals may be false, the masses are ingenuous and sincere: individuals claim the divine sanction of truth for the deceitful conceptions of their own fancies; the Spirit of God breathes through the combined intelligence of the people. Truth is not to be ascertained by the impulses of an individual; it emerges from the contradictions of personal opinions; it raises itself in majestic serenity above the strifes of parties and the conflict of sects; it acknowledges neither the solitary mind, nor the separate faction as its oracle; but owns as its only faithful interpreter the dictates of pure reason itself, proclaimed by the general voice of mankind. The decrees of the universal conscience are the nearest approach to the presence of God in the soul of man.

Thus the opinion which we respect is, indeed, not the opinion of one or of a few, but the sagacity of the many. It is hard for the pride of cultivated philosophy to put its ear to the ground, and listen reverently to the voice of lowly humanity; yet the people collectively are wiser than the most gifted individual, for all his wisdom constitutes but a part of theirs. When the great sculptor of Greece was endeavoring to fashion the perfect model of beauty, he did not passively imitate the form of the loveliest woman of his age; but he gleaned the several lineaments of his faultless work from the many. And so it is, that a perfect judgment is the result of comparison, when error eliminates error, and truth is established by concurring witnesses. The organ of truth is the invisible decision of the unbiased world; she pleads before no tribunal but public opinion; she owns no safe interpreter but the common mind; she knows no court of appeals but the soul of humanity. It is when the multitude give counsel, that right purposes find safety; theirs is the fixedness that cannot be shaken; theirs is the understanding which exceeds in wisdom; theirs is the heart, of which the largeness is as the sand on the sea-shore.

It is not by vast armies, by immense natural resources, by accumulations of treasure, that the greatest results in

modern civilization have been accomplished. The traces of
the career of conquest pass away, hardly leaving a scar
on the national intelligence. The famous battle grounds of
victory are, most of them, comparatively indifferent to
the human race; barren fields of blood, the scourges of
their times, but affecting the social condition as little as
the raging of a pestilence. Not one benevolent institution,
not one ameliorating principle in the Roman state, was a
voluntary concession of the aristocracy; each useful element was borrowed from the Democracies of Greece, or
was a reluctant concession to the demands of the people.
The same is true in modern political life. It is the con-
fession of an enemy to Democracy, that "ALL THE GREAT
AND NOBLE INSTITUTIONS OF THE WORLD HAVE COME
FROM POPULAR EFFORTS."

— Reading No. 14 —

THOMAS DORR: THE RIGHT OF PEOPLE TO REMAKE THEIR CONSTITUTIONS, 1842[14]

*The Constitution of Rhode Island (really the original
charter of 1663) severely limited suffrage to owners of
freehold estates, failed to provide representation for the
fast-growing urban communities of the state, and did not
lend itself to amendment. Despairing of getting any reforms through a narrow and reactionary assembly,
Thomas Dorr, a graduate of Exeter and of Harvard
College, called a people's convention (November 1841)
to draw up a new Constitution. This convention, so Dorr*

[14] From Burke's Report, 28th Congress, 1st Sess., House
Report, 546, pp. 725 ff.

argued, was neither illegal nor revolutionary; it drew its authority from the people who were the source of all political power. When the existing Government of Rhode Island refused to recognize the new Dorr Constitution, Dorr led an abortive revolt. The revolt was speedily put down; Dorr himself was arrested, tried for treason, and sentenced to life imprisonment. Within a year he was released from prison; in 1851 all of his civil rights were restored, and in 1854 the legislature (illegally) annulled the verdict of the court altogether. This statement of the right of the people to take political power back into their own hands is taken from Dorr's speech before the Constitutional Assembly of Rhode Island, May 3, 1842.

✓   ✓   ✓

That the sovereignty of this country resides in the people, is an axiom in the American system of government, too late to be called in question. By the theory of other governments, the sovereign power is vested in the head of the State, or shared with him by the Legislature. The sovereignty of the country from which we derive our origin, and I may add, many of our opinions upon political subjects, inconsistent with our present condition, is in the King and Parliament; and any attempt on the part of the people to change the government of that county, would be deemed an insurrection. There all reform must proceed from the government itself; which calls no conventions of the people, and recognizes no such remedy for political grievances. In this country the case is totally the reverse. When the revolution severed the ties of allegiance, which bound colonies to the parent country, the sovereign power passed from its former possessors, not to the General Government, which was the creation of the States, nor to the State Governments, nor to a portion of the people, but to the whole people of the States, in whom it has ever since remained. This is the doctrine of our fathers, and of the early days of the republic, and should be sacredly guarded as the only safe foundation of our political fabric. The idea that government is in any proper sense the source of power in this country is of foreign origin, and at war with the letter and spirit of our institutions.

The moment we admit the principle, that no change in

government can take place without permission of the existing authorities, we revert to the worn-out theory of the monarchies of Europe; and whether we are the subjects of the Czar of Russia, or of the monarch of Great Britain, or of a landed oligarchy, the difference to us is only in degree, and we have lost the reality, though we may retain the forms of a Democratic Republic. If the people of Rhode Island are wrong in the course they have pursued, they will nevertheless have conferred one benefit upon their countrymen by the agitation of this question, in dissipating the notion that the people are the sovereigns of the country, and in consigning to the department of rhetorical declamation those solemn declarations of 1776, which are repeated in so many of the State Constitutions, and which are so clearly and confidently asserted by the most eminent jurists and statesmen of our country.

If time permitted, I should take great satisfaction in laying before you the most abundant evidence, that these are the well recognized principles of our republican system; and are not to be regarded as revolutionary.

The Declaration of American Independence asserts that governments derive their just powers from the consent of the governed; and that it is the right of the people, meaning the whole people, the governed, to alter or abolish their government whenever they deem it expedient, and to institute new government, laying its foundation on such principles, and organizing its powers in such form, as to them shall seem most likely to effect their safety and happiness. This Declaration was expressly adopted by the General Assembly of this State in July, 1776.

The Constitutions of many of the States, while they contain specific provisions for the mode of their amendment, set forth, in the strongest terms, the right of the people to change them as they may deem expedient. Any other construction would render a portion of the declarations of rights in these Constitutions entirely nugatory.

The Convention which framed the Constitution of the United States, acted as the Representatives of the sovereignty of the people of the States, without regard to the limitation attempted to be imposed by the Congress of the Confederation. That the whole people, by an explicit and authentic act—the great body of society, have a right to make and alter their Constitutions of government, we find ours is a principle which has been laid down by the fathers of the Constitution, and the ablest expounders of our political institutions—by Washington, Hamilton and Madison. The strong opinions of Jefferson on this point are too well known to need a particular repetition.

— Reading No. 15 —

JUSTICE DANIEL: THE RELATION OF PROPERTY TO GOVERNMENT, 1848 [15]

The West River Bridge Company case involved the ever-perplexing problem of the balance between property rights guaranteed under the contract clause of the constitution, and the police power of the state. Under Marshall that balance had been weighted on the side of property rights, especially in the Fletcher v. Peck and the Dartmouth College cases, but even Marshall had recognized that in some circumstances "police power" might take precedence over constitutional limitations. Taney's opinion in the Charles River Bridge Company case of 1837 shifted the center of constitutional gravity to the claims of government. In this notable decision Justice Daniel sustained the right of eminent domain as against the claims of the sanctity of contract.

✦   ✦   ✦

Mr. Justice Daniel delivered the Court's opinion in:

West River Bridge v. *Dix* et al. *Same* v. *Town of Brattleboro* et al. (1848)

[15] From West River Bridge Company *v.* Dix, 6 Howard 532.

The Constitution of the United States, although adopted by the sovereign States of this Union, and proclaimed in its own language to be the Supreme law for their government, can, by no rational interpretation, be brought to conflict with this attribute in the States; there is no express delegation of it by the Constitution; and it would imply an incredible fatuity in the States, to ascribe to them the intention to relinquish the power of self-government and self preservation. A correct view of this matter must demonstrate, moreover, that the right of eminent domain in government in no wise interferes with the inviolability of contracts; that the most sanctimonious regard for the one is perfectly consistent with the possession and exercise of the other.

Under every established government, the tenure of property is derived mediately or immediately from the sovereign power of the political body, organized in such mode or exerted in such way as the community or State may have thought proper to ordain. It can rest on no other guarantee. It is owing to these characteristics only, in the original nation of tenure, that appeals can be made to the laws either for the protection or assertion of the rights of property. Upon any other hypothesis, the law of property would be simply the law of force. Now, it is undeniable that the investment of property in the citizen by the government, whether made for a pecuniary consideration or founded on conditions of civil or political duty, is a contract between the State, or the government acting as its agent, and the grantee; and both the parties thereto are bound in good faith to fulfill it. But into all the contracts, whether made between States and individuals or between individuals only, there enter conditions which arise not out of the literal terms of the contract itself; they are superinduced by the pre-existing and higher authority of the laws of nature, of nations, or of the community to which the parties belong; they are always presumed, and must be presumed to be known and recognized by all, are binding upon all, and need never, therefore, be carried into express stipulation for this could add nothing to their force. Every contract is made in subordination to them, and must yield to their control, as conditions inherent and paramount, wherever a necessity for their execution shall occur. Such a condition is the right of eminent domain. This right does not operate to impair the contract effected by it, but recognizes its obligation in the fullest extent, claiming only the fulfillment of an essential and inseparable condition. . . .

— Reading No. 16 —

MEMORIAL OF THE NON-FREEHOLDERS OF RICHMOND, VIRGINIA, 1829[16]

Virginia's Revolutionary Constitution, too, for all of its liberalism, based suffrage on property, and heavily over-represented the tidewater at the expense of the more westerly counties. The Constitutional Convention of 1829-30—a convention distinguished by the membership of James Madison, James Monroe, John Marshall and Randolph of Roanoke—rejected a proposal for manhood suffrage and retained, instead, a somewhat less burden-some property qualification. Not until 1850 did Virginia do away with the property qualification for suffrage. The Memorial of the Non-Freeholders of Richmond which pleads the case of a democratic suffrage, has a somewhat melancholy interest because it was presented by that arch-conservative Chief Justice John Marshall.

✓   ✓   ✓

The Memorial of the Non-Freeholders of the City of Richmond, respectfully addressed to the Convention, now assembled to deliberate on amendments to the State Constitution:

[16] From *Proceedings and Debates of the Virginia State Convention of 1829-30* (Richmond, Virginia, 1830) p. 25 ff.

Your memorialists, as their designation imports, belong to that class of citizens, who, not having the good fortune to possess a certain portion of land, are, for that cause only, debarred from the enjoyment of the right of suffrage. Experience has but too clearly evinced, what, indeed, reason had always foretold, by how frail a tenure they hold every other right, who are denied this, the highest prerogative of freemen. The want of it has afforded both the pretext and the means of excluding the entire class, to which your memorialists belong, from all participation in the recent election of the body, they now respectfully address. Comprising a very large part, probably a majority of male citizens of mature age, they have been passed by, like aliens or slaves, as if destitute of interest, or unworthy of a voice, in measures involving their future political destiny: whilst the freeholders, sole possessors, under the existing Constitution, of the elective franchise, have, upon the strength of that possession alone, asserted and maintained in themselves, the exclusive power of new-modelling the fundamental laws of the State: in other words, have seized upon the sovereign authority.

It cannot be necessary, in addressing the Convention now assembled, to expatiate on the momentous importance of the right of suffrage, or to enumerate the evils consequent upon its unjust limitation. Were there no other than that your memorialists have brought to your attention, and which has made them feel with full force their degraded condition, well might it justify their best efforts to obtain the great privilege they now seek, as the only effectual method of preventing its recurrence. To that privilege, they respectfully contend, they are entitled equally with its present possessors. Many are bold enough to deny their title. None can show a better. It rests upon no subtle or abstruse reasoning; but upon grounds simple in their character, intelligible to the plainest capacity, and such as appeal to the heart, as well as the understanding, of all who comprehend and duly appreciate the principles of free Government. . . .

Not to the authority of great names merely, does the existing restriction upon suffrage stand opposed: reason and justice equally condemn it. The object, it is presumed, meant to be attained, was, as far as practicable, to admit the meritorious, and reject the unworthy. And had this object really been attained, whatever opinions might prevail as to the mere right, not a murmur probably would have been heard. Surely it were much to be desired that every citizen should be qualified for the proper exercise of all his rights, and the due performance of all his duties. But the same qualifications that entitle him to assume the management of his private affairs, and to claim all other privileges of citizenship, equally entitle him, in the judgment of your memorialists, to be entrusted with this, the dearest of all his privileges, the most important of all his concerns. But if otherwise, still they cannot discern in the possession of land any evidence of peculiar merit, or superior title. To ascribe to a landed possession, moral or intellectual endowments, would truly be regarded as ludicrous, were it not for the gravity with which the proposition is maintained, and still more for the grave consequences flowing from it. Such possession no more proves him who has it, wiser or better, than it proves him taller or stronger, than him who has it not. That cannot be a fit criterion for the exercise of any right, the possession of which does not indicate the existence, nor the want of it the absence, of any essential qualification.

But this criterion, it is strenuously insisted, though not perfect, is yet the best human wisdom can devise. It affords the strongest, if not the only evidence of the requisite qualifications; more particularly of what are absolutely essential, "permanent common interest with, and attachment to, the community." Those who cannot furnish this evidence, are therefore deservedly excluded.

Your memorialists do not design to institute a comparison; they fear none that can be fairly made between the privileged and the proscribed classes. They may be permitted, however, without disrespect, to remark, that of the latter, not a few possess land: many, though not proprietors, are yet cultivators of the soil: others are engaged in avocations of a different nature, often as useful, presupposing no less integrity, requiring as much intelligence, and as fixed a residence, as agricultural pursuits. Virtue, intelligence, are not among the products of the soil. Attachment to property, often a sordid sentiment, is not to be confounded with the sacred flame of patriotism. The love of country, like that of parents and offspring, is engrafted in our nature. It exists in all climates, among all classes, under every possible form of Government. Riches oftener impair it than poverty. Who has it not is a monster. . . .

But, it is said, yield them this right, and they will abuse it: property, that is, landed property, will be rendered insecure, or at least overburthened, by those who possess it not. The freeholders, on the contrary, can pass no law to the injury of any other class, which will not more injuriously affect themselves. The alarm is sounded too, of danger from large manufacturing institutions, where one corrupt individual may sway the corrupt votes of thousands. It were a vain task to attempt to meet all the flimsy pretexts urged, to allay all the apprehensions felt or feigned by the enemies of a just and liberal policy. The danger of abuse is a dangerous plea. Like *necessity,* the detested plea of the tyrant, or the still more detestible plea of the Jesuit, *expediency;* it serves as an ever-ready apology for all oppression. If we are sincerely republican, we must give our confidence to the pri[n]ciples we profess. We have been taught by our fathers, that all power is vested in, and derived from, the people; not the freeholders: that the majority of the community, in whom abides the physical force, have also the political right of creating and remoulding at will, their civil institutions. Nor can this right be any where more safely deposited. The generality of mankind, doubtless, desire to become owners of property: left free to reap the fruit of their labours, they will seek to acquire it honestly. It can never be their interest to overburthen, or render precarious, what they themselves desire to enjoy in peace. But should they ever prove as base as the argument supposes, force alone; arms, not votes, could effect their designs; and when that shall be attempted, what virtue is there in Constitutional restrictions, in mere wax and paper, to withstand it? To deny to the great body of the people all share in the Government; on suspicion that they may deprive others of their property, to rob them, in advance of their rights; to look to a privileged order as the fountain and depository of all power; is to depart from the fundamental maxims, to destroy the chief beauty, the characteristic feature, indeed, of Republican Government. . . .

— Reading No. 17 —

NORTON TOWNSHEND ON NEGRO SUFFRAGE IN OHIO, 1851 [17]

Only in a handful of Northern states, chiefly those of New England, could the free Negro vote before the Civil War. For all its enthusiasm for democracy, Ohio did not permit the free Negro to vote. Dr. Townshend's proposal in the Ohio Constitutional Convention of 1851 to give the vote to free Negroes, was voted down 66-12. The English-born Norton Townshend was something of a universal reformer; he championed not only the cause of the Negro but of women; he was active in Free Soil politics, serving one term in Congress as a Free Soil Democrat; and he worked incessantly for scientific agriculture and agricultural education in Ohio.

✓   ✓   ✓

Feb. 8, 1851

MR. TOWNSHEND. . . .

I am opposed, Mr. President, to the insertion of the word *white* in this Report. The first reason I have to offer for my opposition is the belief that the intended restriction of the right of suffrage is *unjust*.

Sir, I not only say, but I believe that *"all* men are created equal," that is they are equally endowed by their Creator with certain inherent rights. These rights are essential to our existence, they spring from the necessities of our being. In order to live we must have a place somewhere, we must have air and food, and each of these and every other necessity imposed on us by our maker,

[17] From *Report of the Debates and Proceedings of the Convention for the Revision of the Constitution of . . . Ohio, 1850-51* (Columbus, 1851), II, 550-51.

involves a corresponding right whether it pertain to our physical or to our intellectual or moral nature. Some of our rights grow directly out of the relations we sustain, such as husbands or fathers, &c., each of these relations imposing certain obligations or duties, and these involving corresponding rights. All men have by nature the same necessities, and may sustain the same or equal relations, consequently all men must have the same natural rights. For the protection of these natural rights governments are instituted among men, and this single purpose of protection is the only legitimate function of government. All the human governments on earth cannot create a right, nor can they take a right away, and the idea that man on entering into jural or civil relations with these, surrenders any part of his natural rights, is only one of the grand but mischievous blunders of the past. Human governments derive all their just authority from the consent of the governed; all persons have the same rights to protect, and are therefore equally interested, and equally entitled to share as principals in government, and the consent of one person is just as necessary as the consent of another person, in order to constitute just authority.

To attempt to govern men without seeking their consent is usurpation and tyranny, whether in Ohio or in Austria. There is a portion of the people of this State who have the same right to stand upon this part of God's earth, and to breathe this free air, that you or I have, and yet you seek to impose a government upon them without consulting them. I can only say that they are under no obligation to obey your laws or to submit to your authority. You burthen them with taxation without representation, and thus inflict upon them the identical wrong for which the thirteen United Colonies threw off the yoke of the mother country. To establish a government over them, not based on their consent; to subject them to laws they have had no voice in framing; to tax them while you deny them representation is clearly and manifestly unjust; and I might stop here without urging any further objections to the Report, for with governments there should be really but one enquiry, what is just?

Another objection I have to this limitation of the right of suffrage, I believe it is *anti-democratic*. I desire to speak on this point with becoming modesty, for I am but a young man, while I see around me many whose hair has grown gray in the study of democratic principles. One of these gentlemen has said with Jefferson that democracy consists in doing "equal and exact justice to all men," another gentleman has said that democracy concedes to others all it demands for itself, and demands for itself all it concedes to others. If the restriction of the elective franchise is tested by either of these rules it will be found anti-democratic. To justify the practice the report recommends, Jefferson's rule should be amended so as to read 'equal and exact justice to all *white* men—or to all men *except negroes*.' If I understand genuine democracy it is neither more nor less than the golden rule of christianity applied to politics, or to our civil relations— that is doing unto others as we would have others to do unto us, and I see no reason why democracy is not like christianity, comprehensive enough to embrace the whole family of man. I was looking the other day, Mr. President, into Noah Webster's dictionary for the meaning of democracy, and I found as I expected that he defines a democrat to be 'one who favors universal suffrage.' Now some of our friends here have been busy of late in reading out of the democratic party all who did not come up to their standard of democracy. If they were justified in that proceeding I suppose I shall be equally justified in reading them out if they do not come up to this, the true authoritative standard. I should regret to do it, for some of these gentlemen consider themselves pretty good democrats, although in this particular, they are, as I think, behind the times. Nothing is clearer than that genuine democracy must ever be progressive. The rule 'equal and exact justice to all men,' perhaps, can never be amended, but in its application our measures will change from year to year. The evils and abuses to which this rule was first applied, have now, many of them, passed away, but every succeeding age develops abuses requiring new applications of the same rule, and he only is a genuine democrat who faithfully applies this good democratic rule to any new species of abuse or injustice that appears, and not he who having used it once or twice throws it away and uses it no further. I believe it to be our duty here to erect a civil platform upon which the foot of every person in the State may stand and on exactly the same level. I have not intentionally given in this body, one vote, nor do I intend to give one vote, to place any man, or set of men, above the common level. I will vote for no franchise, if by that is meant something which makes one man free to do what may not be done by others. I will vote for no privilege, if by that is meant a private law for the benefit of the few over the many. I will vote for no charters, because I will not by my vote, give to a part by a special grant, what belongs alike to all, and none of these things have any sacredness for me, I will not give the benefit of my vote. I will not give the benefit of holy rood to any hoary abuse, but right the wrong wherever given. But sir, the same sense of justice, which will not permit me from consenting to place another man's foot higher than my own, will also prevent me from consenting to place any man a hair's breadth below the common level. If the government of Ohio is to be in the hands of a privileged class, whether that class be large or small, it will be an aristocracy, a form of government for which I have no partiality; this government ought to be democratic—a government shared by all, for the good of all. Let us then have no limitations of suffrage—for who does not know that such limitations are anti-democratic?

— Reading No. 18 —

ANDREW JACKSON ON ROTATION IN OFFICE, 1829[18]

When Jackson came to the Presidency he found all the posts filled by appointees of predecessors whom he

[18] From Richardson, ed., *Messages and Papers of the Presidents*, Vol. II.

regarded as either hostile to or alien to his own point of view, his interests, and his following. "The late political struggle," he wrote a few days before he took office, "exhibited the people acting against an improper use of the patronage in the hands of the executive branch of the General Govt." Looking upon office as a kind of reward, he thought it improper that his own followers should be denied a share of those rewards; looking upon public service as "plain and simple" he held that if the demands of an office were too exacting for the average American, there was something wrong with the office. What this added up to was an ardent belief in rotation in office: his opponents called it the spoils system. Actually Jackson did not inaugurate the spoils system, nor did he carry it to extremes. Total removals under him came to less than one thousand, and in his eight years in office he replaced only about one-fifth of all office holders.

↗   ↗   ↗

December 8, 1829

*Fellow-Citizen of the Senate and House of
Representatives:*

. . . There are perhaps few men who can for any great length of time enjoy office and power, without being more or less under the influence of feelings unfavorable to the faithful discharge of their public duties. Their integrity may be proof against improper considerations immediately addressed to themselves; but they are apt to acquire a habit of looking with indifference upon the public interests, and of tolerating conduct from which an unpracticed man would revolt. Office is considered as a species of property; and Government rather as a means of promoting individual interests than as an instrument created solely for the service of the People. Corruption in some and in others a perversion of correct feelings and principles divert Government from its legitimate ends, and make it an engine for the support of the few at the expense of the many. The duties of all public officers are, or at least admit of being made, so plain and simple that men of intelligence may readily qualify themselves for their performance; and I cannot but believe that more is lost by the long continuance of men in office than is generally to be gained by their experience. I submit, therefore, to your consideration whether the efficiency of the Government would not be promoted and official industry and integrity better secured by a general extension of the law which limits appointments to four years.

In a country where officers are created solely for the benefit of the people no one man has any more intrinsic right to official station than another. Offices were not established to give support to particular men at the public expense No individual wrong is, therefore, done by removal, since neither appointment to nor continuance in office is matter of right. The incumbent became an officer with a view to public benefits; and when these require his removal they are not to be sacrificed to private interests. It is the People, and they alone, who have a right to complain when a bad officer is substituted for a good one. He who is removed has the same means of obtaining a living that are enjoyed by the millions who never held office. The proposed limitation would destroy the idea of property now so generally connected with official station; and although individual distress may be sometimes produced, it would, by promoting that rotation which constitutes a leading principle in the republican creed, give healthful action to the system. . . .

Andrew Jackson

IV

WOMAN'S RIGHTS

— Reading No. 19 —

CATHERINE BEECHER ON EDUCATION FOR WOMEN, 1829[19]

*The same impulses that led to agitation for the rights
and the welfare of labor, of the Negro, of children, of
the poor, the oppressed, the "dangerous and perishing
classes," excited concern for the rights of women. Perhaps
the most natural expression of this concern was in the
realm of education. By the early years of the 19th century
elementary education for girls was taken for granted
everywhere, and secondary education was available to
some, particularly to the well-to-do. Nowhere, however,
was there any provision for higher education for women.
In 1818 Mrs. Emma Willard proposed to Governor Clin-
ton of New York the establishment of a college for
women; though the State failed to act, the citizens of
Troy provided money for the Troy Female Seminary. The
second pioneer in this field was Catherine Beecher, sister
to Henry Ward Beecher and Harriet Beecher Stowe. In
1824 Miss Beecher founded the Hartford Female Seminary, which soon became a model school of its kind. Miss*

[19] From Catherine Beecher, "Suggestions Respecting Improve-
    ments in Education, Presented to the Trustees of the
    Hartford Female Seminary" (1829) in H. S. Commager,
    ed., *Living Ideas in America* (New York, 1951) 564 ff.

Beecher eventually helped found a series of seminaries and colleges for women throughout the country. We give here a brief excerpt from her "Suggestions" on how to improve education for women.

✓   ✓   ✓

It is to *mothers,* and to *teachers,* that the world is to look for the character which is to be enstamped on each succeeding generation, for it is to them that the great business of education is almost exclusively committed. And will it not appear by examination that neither mothers nor teachers have ever been properly educated for their profession. What is *the profession* of a *Woman*? Is it not to form immortal minds, and to watch, to nurse, and to rear the bodily system, so fearfully and wonderfully made, and upon the order and regulation of which, the health and well-being of the mind so greatly depends?

But let most of our sex upon whom these arduous duties devolve, be asked; have you ever devoted any time and study, in the course of your education, to any preparation for these duties? Have you been taught any thing of the structure, the nature, and the laws of the body, which you inhabit? Were you ever taught to understand the operation of diet, air, exercise and modes of dress upon the human frame? Have the causes which are continually operating to prevent good health, and the modes by which it might be perfected and preserved ever been made the subject of any *instruction?* Perhaps almost every voice would respond, no; we have attended to almost every thing more than to this; we have been taught more concerning the structure of the earth; the laws of the heavenly bodies; the habits and formation of plants; the philosophy of languages; more of *almost any thing,* than the structure of the human frame and the laws of health and reason. But is it not the business, the *profession* of a woman to guard the health and form the physical habits of the young? And is not the cradle of infancy and the chamber of sickness sacred to woman alone? And ought she not to know at least some of the *general principles* of that perfect and wonderful piece of mechanism committed to her preservation and care?

The *restoration* of health is the physician's profession, but the *preservation* of it falls to other hands, and it is believed that the time will come, when woman will be taught to understand something respecting the construction of the human frame; the physiological results which will naturally follow from restricted exercise, unhealthy modes of dress, improper diet, and many other causes, which are continually operating to destroy the health and life of the young.

Again let our sex be asked respecting the instruction they have received in the course of their education, on that still more arduous and difficult department of their profession, which relates to the *intellect* and the *moral susceptibilities*. Have you been taught the powers and faculties of the human mind, and the laws by which it is regulated? Have you studied how to direct its several faculties; how to restore those that are overgrown, and strengthen and mature those that are deficient? Have you been taught the best modes of *communicating* knowledge as well as of *acquiring* it? Have you learned the best mode of correcting bad *moral* habits and forming good ones? Have you made it an object to find how a selfish disposition may be made generous; how a reserved temper may be made open and frank; how pettishness and ill humor may be changed to cheerfulness and kindness? Has any woman studied her profession in this respect? It is feared the same answer must be returned, if not from all, at least from most of our sex. No; we have acquired wisdom from the observation and experience of others, on almost *all other* subjects, but the philosophy of the direction and control of the human mind has not been an object of thought or study. And thus it appears that tho' it is woman's *express business* to rear the body, and form the mind, there is scarcely anything to which her attention has been less directed. . . .

If all females were not only well educated themselves, but were prepared to communicate in an easy manner their stores of knowledge to others; if they not only knew how to regulate their own minds, tempers and habits, but how to effect improvements in those around them, the face of society would speedily be changed. The time *may* come when the world will look back with wonder to behold how much time and effort have been given to the mere cultivation of the memory, and how little mankind have been aware of what every teacher, parent, and friend could accomplish in forming the social, intellectual and moral character of those by whom they are surrounded.

— Reading No. 20 —

SENECA FALLS DECLARATION OF INDEPENDENCE, 1848 [20]

The movement for woman's rights grew out of the antislavery struggle, for when women found themselves excluded from the platform of abolitionist meetings they discovered that they, too, needed emancipation. The Seneca Falls Convention on woman's rights—and wrongs —was called by Lucretia Mott and Elizabeth Cady Stanton; its Declaration of Sentiments, modelled on the Declaration of Independence, is the real beginning of the woman's rights movement in the United States.

✓   ✓   ✓

1. DECLARATION OF SENTIMENTS

When, in the course of human events, it becomes necessary for one portion of the family of man to assume among the people of the earth a position different from that which they have hitherto occupied, but one to which the laws of nature and of nature's God entitle them, a decent respect to the opinions of mankind requires that they should declare the causes that impel them to such a course.

We hold these truths to be self-evident: that all men and women are created equal; that they are endowed by their Creator with certain inalienable rights; that among these are life, liberty, and the pursuit of happiness; that to secure these rights governments are instituted, deriving

[20] From H. S. Commager, ed., *Documents of American History* (New York, 1958) Doc. No. 172.

their just powers from the consent of the governed. Whenever any form of government becomes destructive of these ends, it is the right of those who suffer from it to refuse allegiance to it, and to insist upon the institution of a new government, laying its foundation on such principles, and organizing its powers in such form, as to them shall seem most likely to effect their safety and happiness. Prudence, indeed, will dictate that governments long established should not be changed for light and transient causes; and accordingly all experience hath shown that mankind are more disposed to suffer while evils are sufferable, than to right themselves by abolishing the forms to which they are accustomed. But when a long train of abuses and usurpations, pursuing invariably the same object, evinces a design to reduce them under absolute despotism, it is their duty to throw off such government, and to provide new guards for their future security. Such has been the patient sufferance of the women under this government, and such is now the necessity which constrains them to demand the equal station to which they are entitled.

The history of mankind is a history of repeated injuries and usurpations on the part of man toward woman, having in direct object the establishment of an absolute tyranny over her. To prove this, let facts be submitted to a candid world.

He has never permitted her to exercise her inalienable right to the elective franchise.

He has compelled her to submit to laws, in the formation of which she had no voice.

He has withheld from her rights which are given to the most ignorant and degraded men—both natives and foreigners.

Having deprived her of this first right of a citizen, the elective franchise, thereby leaving her without representation in the halls of legislation, he has oppressed her on all sides.

He has made her, if married, in the eye of the law, civilly dead.

He has taken from her all right in property, even to the wages she earns.

He has made her, morally, an irresponsible being, as she can commit many crimes with impunity, provided they be done in the presence of her husband. In the covenant of marriage, she is compelled to promise obedience to her husband, he becoming, to all intents and purposes, her master—the law giving him power to deprive her of her liberty, and to administer chastisement.

He has so framed the laws of divorce, as to what shall be the proper causes, and in case of separation, to whom the guardianship of the children shall be given, as to be wholly regardless of the happiness of women—the law, in all cases, going upon a false supposition of the supremacy of man, and giving all power into his hands.

After depriving her of all rights as a married woman, if single, and the owner of property, he has taxed her to support a government which recognizes her only when her property can be made profitable to it.

He has monopolized nearly all the profitable employments, and from those she is permitted to follow, she receives but a scanty remuneration. He closes against her all the avenues to wealth and distinction which he considers most honorable to himself. As a teacher of theology, medicine, or law, she is not known.

He has denied her the facilities for obtaining a thorough education, all colleges being closed against her.

He allows her in Church, as well as State, but a subordinate position, claiming Apostolic authority for her exclusion from the ministry, and, with some exceptions, from any public participation in the affairs of the Church.

He has created a false public sentiment by giving to the world a different code of morals for men and women, by which moral delinquencies which exclude women from society, are not only tolerated, but deemed of little account in man.

He has usurped the prerogative of Jehovah himself, claiming it as his right to assign for her a sphere of action, when that belongs to her conscience and to her God.

He has endeavored, in every way that he could, to destroy her confidence in her own powers, to lessen her self-respect and to make her willing to lead a dependent and abject life.

Now, in view of this entire disfranchisement of one-half the people of this country, their social and religious degradation—in view of the unjust laws above mentioned, and because women do feel themselves aggrieved, oppressed, and fraudulently deprived of their most sacred rights, we insist that they have immediate admission to all the rights and privileges which belong to them as citizens of the United States.

In entering upon the great work before us, we anticipate no small amount of misconception, misrepresentation, and ridicule; but we shall use every instrumentality within our power to effect our object. We shall employ agents, circulate tracts, petition the State and National legislatures, and endeavor to enlist the pulpit and the press in our behalf. We hope this Convention will be followed by a series of Conventions embracing every part of the country.

2. RESOLUTIONS

Whereas, The great precept of nature is conceded to be, that "man shall pursue his own true and substantial happiness." Blackstone in his Commentaries remarks, that this law of Nature being coeval with mankind, and dictated by God himself, is of course superior in obligation to any other. It is binding over all the globe, in all countries and at all times; no human laws are of any validity if contrary to this, and such of them as are valid, derive all their force, and all their validity, and all their authority, mediately and immediately, from this original; therefore,

Resolved, That all laws which prevent woman from occupying such a station in society as her conscience shall dictate, or which place her in a position inferior to that of man, are contrary to the great precept of nature, and therefore of no force or authority.

Resolved, That woman is man's equal—was intended to be so by the Creator, and the highest good of the race demands that she should be recognized as such.

Resolved, That the women of this country ought to be enlightened in regard to the laws under which they live, that they may no longer publish their degradation by declaring themselves satisfied with their present position, nor their ignorance, by asserting that they have all the rights they want.

Resolved, That inasmuch as man, while claiming for himself intellectual superiority, does accord to woman moral superiority, it is pre-eminently his duty to encourage her to speak and teach, as she has an opportunity, in all religious assemblies.

Resolved, That the same amount of virtue, delicacy, and refinement of behavior that is required of woman in the social state, should also be required of man, and the same transgressions should be visited with equal severity on both man and woman.

Resolved, That the objection of indelicacy and impropriety, which is so often brought against woman when she addresses a public audience, comes with a very ill-grace from those who encourage, by their attendance, her appearance on the stage, in the concert, or in feats of the circus.

Resolved, That woman has too long rested satisfied in the circumscribed limits which corrupt customs and a perverted application of the Scriptures have marked out for her, and that it is time she should move in the enlarged sphere which her great Creator has assigned her.

Resolved, That it is the duty of the women of this country to secure to themselves their sacred rights to the elective franchise. . . .

Resolved, That the speedy success of our cause depends upon the zealous and untiring efforts of both men and women, for the overthrow of the monopoly of the pulpit, and for the securing to women an equal participation with men in the various trades, professions and commerce.

Resolved, therefore, That, being invested by the creator with the same capabilities, and the same consciousness of responsibility for their exercise, it is demonstrably the right and duty of woman, equally with man, to promote every righteous cause by every righteous means; and especially in regard to the great subjects of morals and religion, it is self-evidently her right to participate with her brother in teaching them, both in private and in public, by writing and by speaking, by any instrumentalities proper to be used, and in any assemblies proper to be held; and this being a self-evident truth growing out of the divinely implanted principles of human nature, any custom or authority adverse to it, whether modern or wearing the hoary sanction of antiquity, is to be regarded as a self-evident falsehood, and at war with mankind.

— Reading No. 21 —

LUCY STONE: PROTEST AGAINST EXISTING MARRIAGE RULES AND CUSTOMS, 1855 [21]

Lucy Stone was one of the earliest, and long one of the most effective and distinguished champions of woman's rights. She had worked her way through Mt. Holyoke Seminary, and Oberlin College; then participated in the antislavery crusade, and from that moved into the woman's rights movement. In 1855 she married Henry Brown Blackwell—whose brother had married the ardent feminist Antoinette Brown—on condition that he permit her to keep her maiden name, and that he devote himself to the crusade for woman's rights. For the next thirty years Lucy Stone and her husband worked incessantly—and on the whole successfully—for the cause they had at heart.

✓　　　　✓　　　　✓

MARRIAGE OF LUCY STONE UNDER PROTEST

It was my privilege to celebrate May day by officiating at a wedding in a farm-house among the hills of West Brookfield. The bridegroom was a man of tried worth, a leader in the Western Anti-Slavery Movement; and the bride was one whose fair name is known throughout the nation; one whose rare intellectual qualities are excelled by the private beauty of her heart and life.

I never perform the marriage ceremony without a renewed sense of the iniquity of our present system of laws in respect to marriage; a system by which "man and wife are one, and that one is the husband." It was with my hearty concurrence, therefore, that the following protest was read and signed, as a part of the nuptial ceremony; and I send it to you, that others may be induced to do likewise.

REV. THOMAS WENTWORTH HIGGINSON.

[21] From Elizabeth Cady Stanton, *et al.*, eds., *History of Woman Suffrage* (Rochester, 1887) I, 260-61.

PROTEST

While acknowledging our mutual affection by publicly assuming the relation of husband and wife, yet in justice to ourselves and a great principle, we deem it a duty to declare that this act on our part implies no sanction of, nor promise of voluntary obedience to such of the present laws of marriage, as refuse to recognize the wife as an independent, rational being, while they confer upon the husband an injurious and unnatural superiority, investing him with legal powers which no honorable man would exercise, and which no man should possess. We protest especially against the laws which give to the husband:

1. The custody of the wife's person.

2. The exclusive control and guardianship of their children.

3. The sole ownership of her personal, and use of her real estate, unless previously settled upon her, or placed in the hands of trustees, as in the case of minors, lunatics, and idiots.

4. The absolute right to the product of her industry.

5. Also against laws which give to the widower so much larger and more permanent an interest in the property of his deceased wife, than they give to the widow in that of the deceased husband.

6. Finally, against the whole system by which "the legal existence of the wife is suspended during marriage," so that in most States, she neither has a legal part in the choice of her residence, nor can she make a will, nor sue or be sued in her own name, nor inherit property.

We believe that personal independence and equal human rights can never be forfeited, except for crime; that marriage should be an equal and permanent partnership, and so recognized by law; that until it is so recognized, married partners should provide against the radical injustice of present laws, by every means in their power.

We believe that where domestic difficulties arise, no appeal should be made to legal tribunals under existing laws, but that all difficulties should be submitted to the equitable adjustment of arbitrators mutually chosen.

Thus reverencing law, we enter our protest against

rules and customs which are unworthy of the name, since they violate justice, the essence of law.

HENRY B. BLACKWELL,
LUCY STONE.

Worcester Spy, 1855.

— Reading No. 22 —

OHIO MEMORIAL ON WOMAN SUFFRAGE, 1850[22]

Agitation for political and legal rights of women began in Ohio in the late 'forties; Oberlin College was the first of the "co-educational" colleges; and both Lucy Stone and Antoinette Brown studied there. In April 1850 a convention of slavery and woman's rights reformers met at Salem, Ohio, and memorialized the Ohio Constitutional Convention on behalf of the vote and of legal and property rights for women. The Convention rejected these proposals by a resounding vote of 72-7.

✦   ✦   ✦

MEMORIAL

We believe the whole theory of the Common Law in relation to woman is unjust and degrading, tending to reduce her to a level with the slave, depriving her of political existence, and forming a positive exception to the great doctrine of equality as set forth in the Declaration of Independence. In the language of Prof. Walker, in his "Introduction to American Law": "Women have no part or lot in the foundation or administration of the government. They can not vote or hold office. They are required to contribute their share, by way of taxes, to the

[22] From Elizabeth Cady Stanton, *et al.,* eds., *History of Woman Suffrage* (Rochester, 1887) I, 105.

support of the Government, but are allowed no voice in
its direction. They are amenable to the laws, but are allowed no share in making them. This language, when
applied to males, would be the exact definition of political slavery." Is it just or wise that woman, in the
largest and professedly the freest and most enlightened
republic on the globe, in the middle of the nineteenth
century, should be thus degraded?

We would especially direct the attention of the Convention to the legal condition of married women. Not
being represented in those bodies from which emanate
the laws, to which they are obliged to submit, they are
protected neither in person nor property. "The merging
of woman's name in that of her husband is emblematical
of the fate of all her legal rights." At the marriage-altar,
the law divests her of all distinct individuality. Blackstone says: "The very being or legal existence of the
woman is suspended during marriage, or at least incorporated or consolidated into that of her husband." Legally, she ceases to exist, and becomes emphatically a
new creature, and is ever after denied the dignity of a
rational and accountable being. The husband is allowed
to take possession of her estates, as the law has proclaimed
her legally dead. All that she has, becomes legally his,
and he can collect and dispose of the profits of her labor
without her consent, as he thinks fit, and she can own
nothing, have nothing, which is not regarded by the law
as belonging to her husband. Over her person he has a
more limited power. Still, if he render life intolerable,
so that she is forced to leave him, he has the power to
retain her children, and "seize her and bring her back,
for he has a right to her society which he may enforce,
either against herself or any other person who detains
her." Woman by being thus subject to the control, and
dependent on the will of man, loses her self-dependence;
and no human being can be deprived of this without a
sense of degradation. The law should sustain and protect
all who come under its sway, and not create a state of dependence and depression in any human being. The laws
should not make woman a mere pensioner on the bounty
of her husband, thus enslaving her will and degrading her
to a condition of absolute dependence.

Believing that woman does not suffer alone when subject to oppressive and unequal laws, but that whatever
affects injuriously her interests, is subversive of the highest good of the race, we earnestly request that in the New
Constitution you are about to form for the State of Ohio,
women shall be secured, not only the right of suffrage,
but all the political and legal rights that are guaranteed
to men.

— Reading No. 23 —

WENDELL PHILLIPS: PLEA FOR WOMAN SUFFRAGE, 1861 [23]

*There was an interlocking directorate of reformers,
especially in New England, and many of the leaders of
the antislavery struggle, or the humanitarian crusade,
were active in the movement for woman's rights: Garrison, T. W. Higginson, Theodore Parker, among others.*

*Wendell Phillips, a member of one of New England's
first families, had been brought into the antislavery movement at the time of the Faneuil Hall protest against the
murder of Elijah Lovejoy; three years later he joined
Garrison in an effort to grant equality to women at the
World's Anti-Slavery Convention in London. From then
on he devoted his talents and his eloquence to the crusade
for woman's rights.*

✓   ✓   ✓

What proves the clearest woman's need of the ballot?
Why, the very inertness and ignorance which the lack
of it has caused her. Like all other injustice and slavery,

[23] From Wendell Phillips, "Woman's Rights and Woman's
Duties," in *Speeches, Lectures and Letters, Second Series*
(Boston, 1891) 121-4.

its worst effect is that it weakens, degrades, and darkens
its victims, till they no longer realize the harm done
them. Wasted on trifles, cramped by routine, lacking the
stir and breadth which interest in great questions gives,
many women grope or flutter on, ignorant of the real
cause that saddens their life, burdens their toil, starves
their nature, and sows their path with thorns. Those
whom circumstances have lifted to broader views must
not wait for her request before they open to woman the
advantages by which they have profited so much. Besides,
we lose half our resources when we shut women out from
beneath the influence of these elements of growth. God
gives us the whole race with its varied endowments, man
and woman, one the complement of the other, on which
to base civilization. We starve ourselves by using in civil
affairs only half—only one sex. I spoke a year ago of
the stride literature made when women began to write
and read. Politics will reap as great a gain when she
enters its field.

I mean to get the ballot for women—why? Because
Republicanism demands it; because the theory of our
institutions demands it; because the moral health of the
country demands it. What is our Western civilization in
this State of New York, in this city of New York? A
failure! As Humboldt well said, as Earl Gray has said
in the House of Lords, "The experiment of American
government is a failure to-day." It cannot be denied. If
this is the best that free institutions can do, then just as
good, and a great deal better, can be done by despotism.
The city of Paris to-day, with but one will in it, that of
Napoleon, spends less, probably, than the city of New
York spends, and the results are, comfort, safety, health,
quiet, peace, beauty, civilization. New York, governed by
brothels and grog-shops, spends twenty-five per cent more,
and the results are, murder, drunkenness, rowdyism, un-
safety, dirt, and disgrace! I think there is something to
be said for despotism in that point of view. I weigh Paris,
the representative of despotism, against New York, the
representative of "Young America," and New York kicks
the beam. No man can deny it. It is a failure on two
grounds,—it is a failure, because the law of political
economy has given to man good wages, and science has

invented for him drink cheap as water, and held it to his lips, and said, "Make a brute of yourself!"

Give men fair wages, and ninety-nine out of a hundred will disdain to steal. The way to prevent dishonesty is to let every man have a field for his work, and honest wages; the way to prevent licentiousness is to give to woman's capacity free play. Give to the higher powers activity, and they will choke down the animal. The man who loves thinking, disdains to be the victim of appetite. It is a law of our nature. Give a hundred women honest wages for capacity and toil, and ninety-nine will disdain to win it by vice. That is the cure for licentiousness.

V

ECONOMIC REFORM

— Reading No. 24 —

THOMAS SKIDMORE: A PLAN FOR EQUALIZING PROPERTY, 1829[24]

There were, in effect, two reform movements, the one religious and philosophical, the other secular and practical. The first stemmed largely from Boston, Cambridge and Concord, from Harvard and the Unitarian Church, and concerned itself with problems of spiritual progress,

[24] From Thomas Skidmore, *The Rights of Man to Property* (New York, 1829) 125 ff.

*intellectual freedom, and humanitarianism. The second
stemmed rather from New York, and addressed itself
more to the welfare of the workingmen, of the landless,
of immigrants, to problems of banks and money. To be
sure, the two streams of reform often flowed in the same
channel: a Parker, a Howe, a Phillips championed the
cause of the underprivileged in all fields; a Greeley, a
Tappan, a Gerritt Smith, was deeply involved in antislavery and humanitarian reforms.*

*Much of the agitation of this generation was concerned
with the oppression of workingmen; the right of access
to public land; the issue of monopoly, especially in banking, and similar questions. The solutions proposed were
often radical and sometimes downright anarchical. They
were, however, animated by a passionate concern with
the welfare of the underprivileged and by an infinite
faith in progress through mechanical devices. One of the
most ardent reformers was Thomas Skidmore, an asso-
ciate of Frances Wright in the short-lived Workingmen's
Party in New York in the late 'twenties. He advocated
a ten hour day for workers; the end of monopoly in land;
the end of inheritance; and universal education. His
treatise* The Rights of Man to Property *sets forth his
program in detail.*

✓   ✓   ✓

PLAN

1. Let a new State Convention be assembled. Let it
prepare a new constitution, and let that constitution, after
having been adopted by the people, decree an abolition
of all debts, both at home and abroad, between citizen and
citizen, and between citizen and foreigner. Let it renounce
all property belonging to our citizens, without the State.
Let it claim all property within the State, both real and
personal, of whatever kind it may be, with the exception
of that belonging to resident aliens, and with the further
exception of so much personal property as may be in the
possession of transient owners, not being citizens. Let it
order an equal division of all this property among the
citizens, of and over the age of maturity, in manner yet
to be directed. Let it order all transfers or removals of
property, except so much as may belong to transient
owners, to cease until the division is accomplished.

2. Let a census be taken of the people, ascertaining and recording in books made for the purpose the name, time when born, as near as may be, and annexing the age, the place of nativity, parentage, sex, color, occupation, domicile or residence, and time of residence since last resident in the State, distinguishing aliens from citizens, and ordering, with the exception of the Agents of Foreign Governments, such as Ambassadors, etc., that all such aliens shall be considered as citizens if they have been resident for the five years next previous to the time when the before mentioned division of property shall have been ordered.

3. Let each citizen, association, corporation, and other persons at the same time when the census is being taken give an inventory of all personal property, of whatever description it may be, and to whomsoever it may belong, in his, her, or their possession. Let also a similar inventory of all real property within the State be taken, whoever may be the owner of it. And from these data let a general inventory be made out of all the real and personal property within the State which does not belong to alien residents or transient owners. To this let there be added all property in the possession of our tribunals of law and equity, and such State property as can be offered up to sale without detriment to the State.

4. Let there be next a dividend made of this amount among all such citizens who shall be of and over the age of eighteen, if this should be fixed as I am inclined to think it should be as the age of maturity; and let such dividend be entered in a book for the purpose to the credit of such persons, male and female.

5. Let public sale be made, as soon after such dividend is made as may be practicable, to the highest bidder of all the real and personal property in the State. Care must be taken that the proper authority be required to divide all divisible property that shall require it into such allotments or parcels as will be likely to cause it to bring the greatest amount at the time of sale.

6. All persons having such credit, on the books before mentioned, are authorized and required to bid for an amount of property falling short not more than ten per cent. of the sum placed to their credit and not exceeding it more than ten per cent. Delivery may be made of the

whole, if it be real property, and the receiver may stand charged with the overplus. If it be personal property, delivery to be made only to the amount of the dividend unless it be secured.

7. When property, real or personal, is offered for sale which is not in its nature divisible and in its value such as to be of an amount greater than would fall to the lot of any one person, then it shall be proper to receive a joint bid of two or more persons, and these may purchase in conjunction, giving in their names, however, at the time of sale.

8. As it regards personal property which may be secreted or clandestinely put out of the way, order should be given that from the time when any Inventory of any person's property of the kind is made out up to the completion of the General Sale, the owner should be answerable for the forthcoming of so much as may be left in his possession, at the peril of imprisonment for fourteen years, as is now the punishment for the crime of grand larceny, unless good cause were shown to the contrary. Similar punishment, also, should be visited upon everyone who knowingly gave in a false or defective statement of the property he had in his possession or who, having received his patrimony, goes abroad and receives debts or property which the State has renounced.

9. As the General Sales are closed, their amount should be ascertained, and a new dividend declared. It will then be seen how much this dividend, which may be called a "patrimony," differs from the original dividend. By comparing the amount of each person's purchases with this patrimony, it will be seen whether he is creditor or debtor to the State, and how much, and he will be entitled to receive the same or required to pay it to the State accordingly.

10. There is one exception to the delivering of property to persons who may bid it off. It is to those for whom, from excessive intemperance, insanity, or other incapacitating cause, the law may provide, as it should, proper and suitable trustees or guardians. Under proper regulations, it should be entrusted to *them*.

11. While all this is transacting, persons already arrived at the age of maturity and before they can be put in possession of their own patrimony will die. Of these

and others throughout the State, a daily register should be kept from this time forward forever; and so also should be kept another register of the births of those now in minority and of those that shall hereafter be born. The property intended to be given to those who shall thus have died and the property of those who shall have received their patrimony in consequence of the General Division and who shall die before the first day of January ensuing the completion of the General Sales shall be divided equally among all those who shall have arrived at the age of maturity between the time of taking the Census aforesaid and the first day of January just mentioned.

12. An annual dividend forever shall be made of the property left throughout the State by persons dying between the last day of every year and the first day of the next succeeding among those who throughout the State, male and female, shall have arrived at the age of maturity within such period; and it shall be at their option, after the dividend is made, to receive it in cash or to use the credit of it in the future purchase of other property which the State will have constantly on sale in consequence of the decease of other persons in the ensuing year.

13. Property belonging to persons not citizens, but transiently resident among us, and dying here, to abide by the laws which govern the state or nation to which such person belonged in the disposal of property in such a situation; provided such state or nation allows the property, or the value thereof, of our citizens dying there and leaving property to be sent home to abide by the operation of our own laws.

14. Other states or nations adopting a similar internal organization as it regards the transmission of property to posterity, and consenting to bestow patrimonies upon minors born in this State—and who shall prefer receiving them in any such foreign state—upon their producing documents certifying the fact of their nativity, age, etc., and that they have received no patrimony from their native state, shall have the favor reciprocated under like circumstances; otherwise, a minor born in another state must reside the last ten years of his minority in this before he can be considered as entitled to the patrimony of a native born citizen, and must moreover be liable to

severe punishment if, either after he has received his patrimony, he accepts aught from his native or other state, by way of legacy or gift, or, before maturity, he receives such legacy or gift, and then accepts the patrimony in question.

15. All persons of full age from abroad, Ambassadors, etc., excepted, resident one year among us, are citizens and must give up all property over an amount equal to the patrimony of the State for the year being, unless such persons were citizens of a state acknowledging the equal rights of all men to property in manner the same as this State is supposed to do.

16. All native born citizens from the period of their birth to that of their maturity shall receive from the State a sum paid monthly or other more convenient installments equal to their full and decent maintenance according to age and condition; and the parent or parents, if living and not rendered unsuitable by incapacity or vicious habits to train up their children, shall be the persons authorized to receive it. Otherwise, guardians must be appointed to take care of such children and receive their maintenance allowance. They are to be educated also at the public expense.

17. When the death happens of either of any two married persons, the survivor retains one half of the sum of their joint property, their debts being first paid. The other half goes to the State, through the hands of the Public Administrator; this Office taking charge of the effects of all deceased persons.

18. Punishment by imprisonment for a term of fourteen years should be visited upon him who during his lifetime gives away his property to another. Hospitality is, of course, not interdicted but charity is, inasmuch as ample provision will be made by the State for such persons as shall require it. The good citizen has only to inform the applicant for charity where his proper wants will be supplied.

19. All persons after receiving their patrimony will be at full liberty to reside within the State, or to take it or its avails to any other part of the world which may be preferred and there to reside as a citizen or subject of another state.

20. Property being thus continually and equally di-

vided forever, and the receivers of such property embarking in all the various pursuits and occupations of life, these pursuits and occupations must be guaranteed against injury from foreign competition, or otherwise indemnity should be made by the State.

I have thus developed the principles of the modification which the Government of this State should undergo and the means necessary to accomplish it in order that every citizen may enjoy in a state of society substantially the rights which belong to him in a state of nature. I leave the reader therefore for the present to his own reflections, intending in the next chapter to offer such reasons as the subject admits for enforcing the propriety of adopting such modification and of the means proposed of accomplishing it.

— Reading No. 25 —

WILLIAM LEGGETT: RICH AND POOR, 1834[25]

When in 1829 the poet William Cullen Bryant took over the famous New York Evening Post, *he called the young poet, story-teller, and publicist William Leggett to be assistant editor. An ardent Jacksonian, and an inveterate enemy of banks and bankers, and of all forms of special privilege, Leggett soon made himself the leader of the left wing or Loco Foco branch of the New York Democracy. A violent temper and intellectual vagaries made him, however, ineffective as a political leader. During his short life he wrote prodigiously; from his writings his friend Theodore Sedgwick of the powerful Sedgwick clan, selected materials for a two volume edition of po-*

[25] From William Leggett, *A Collection of the Political Writings* (New York, 1840) I, 106 ff.

*litical writings. It is from these that we take this editorial
on the rich and the poor.*

✓   ✓   ✓

RICH AND POOR

The rich perceive, acknowledge, and act upon a common interest, and why not the poor? Yet the moment the
latter are called upon to combine for the preservation of
their rights, forsooth the community is in danger. Property is no longer secure and life in jeopardy. This cant
has descended to us from those times when the poor and
laboring classes had no stake in the community and no
rights except such as they could acquire by force. But
the times have changed though the cant remains the same.
The scrip nobility of this Republic have adopted towards
the free people of this Republic the same language which
the feudal barons and the despot who contested with
them the power of oppressing the people used towards
their serfs and villains, as they were opprobriously called.

These would-be lordlings of the Paper Dynasty cannot
or will not perceive that there is some difference in the
situation and feelings of the people of the United States
and those of the despotic governments of Europe. They
forget that at this moment our people—we mean emphatically the class which labors with its own hands—is
in possession of a greater portion of the property and
intelligence of this country, ay, ten times over, than all
the creatures of the "paper credit system" put together.
This property is indeed more widely and equally distributed among the people than among the phantoms of the
paper system, and so much the better. And as to their
intelligence, let any man talk with them, and if he does
not learn something it is his own fault. They are as well
acquainted with the rights of person and property and
have as just a regard for them as the most illustrious
lordling of the scrip nobility. And why should they not?
Who and what are the great majority of the wealthy people of this city, we may say of this country? Are they
not—we say it not in disparagement, but in high com-
mendation—are they not men who began the world comparatively poor with ordinary education and ordinary
means? And what should make them so much wiser than

their neighbors? Is it because they live in better style, ride in carriages, and have more money or at least more credit than their poorer neighbors? Does a man become wiser, stronger, or more virtuous and patriotic because he has a fine house over his head? Does he love his country the better because he has a French cook and a box at the opera? Or does he grow more learned, logical, and profound by intense study of the daybook, ledger, bills of exchange, bank promises, and notes of hand?

Of all the countries on the face of the earth or that ever existed on the face of the earth, this is the one where the claims of wealth and aristocracy are the most unfounded, absurd, and ridiculous. With no claim to hereditary distinctions, with no exclusive rights except what they derive from monopolies, and no power of perpetuating their estates in their posterity, the assumption of aristocratic airs and claims is supremely ridiculous. Tomorrow they themselves may be beggars for aught they know, or at all events their children may become so. Their posterity in the second generation will have to begin the world again and work for a living as did their forefathers. And yet the moment a man becomes rich among us, he sets up for wisdom; he despises the poor and ignorant; he sets up for patriotism; he is your only man who has a stake in the community and therefore the only one who ought to have a voice in the state. What folly is this? And how contemptible his presumption? He is not a whit wiser, better, or more patriotic than when he commenced the world, a wagon driver. Nay, not half so patriotic, for he would see his country disgraced a thousand times rather than see one fall of the stocks, unless perhaps he had been speculating on such a contingency. To him a victory is only of consequence as it raises, and a defeat only to be lamented as it depresses a loan. His soul is wrapped up in a certificate of scrip or a bank note. Witness the conduct of these pure patriots during the late war, when they, at least a large proportion of them, not only withheld all their support from the Government but used all their influence to prevent others from giving their assistance. Yet these are the people who alone have a stake in the community and, of course, exclusively monopolize patriotism.

But let us ask what and where is the danger of a com-

bination of the laboring classes in vindication of their
political principles or in defense of their menaced rights?
Have they not the right to act in concert when their opponents act in concert? Nay, is it not their bounden duty
to combine against the only enemy they have to fear as
yet in this free country: monopoly and a great paper
system that grinds them to the dust? Truly, this is strange
republican doctrine, and this is a strange republican
country, where men cannot unite in one common effort,
in one common cause, without rousing the cry of danger
to the rights of person and property. Is not this a government of the people, founded on the rights of the people, and instituted for the express object of guarding
them against the encroachments and usurpations of
power? And if they are not permitted the possession of
common interest, the exercise of a common feeling, if
they cannot combine to resist by constitutional means
these encroachments, to what purpose were they declared
free to exercise the right of suffrage in the choice of
rulers and the making of laws?

And what, we ask, is the power against which the people not only of this country but of almost all Europe are
called upon to array themselves, and the encroachment
on their rights they are summoned to resist? Is it not
emphatically the power of monopoly and the encroachments of corporate privileges of every kind which the
cupidity of the rich engenders to the injury of the poor?

It was to guard against the encroachments of power,
the insatiate ambition of wealth, that this government was
instituted by the people themselves. But the objects which
call for the peculiar jealousy and watchfulness of the
people are not now what they once were. The cautions
of the early writers in favor of the liberties of mankind
have in some measure become obsolete and inapplicable.
We are menaced by our old enemies, avarice and ambition, under a new name and form. The tyrant is changed
from a steel-clad feudal baron or a minor despot, at the
head of thousands of ruffian followers, to a mighty civil
gentleman who comes mincing and bowing to the people
with a quill behind his ear, at the head of countless millions of magnificent *promises*. He promises to make
everybody rich; he promises to pave cities with gold; and
he promises to pay. In short he is made up of promises.

He will do wonders such as never were seen or heard of, provided the people will only allow him to make his promises equal to silver and gold and human labor, and grant him the exclusive benefits of all the great blessings he intends to confer on them. He is the sly, selfish, grasping, and insatiable tyrant the people are now to guard against. A *concentrated money power;* a usurper in the disguise of a benefactor; an agent exercising privileges which his principal never possessed; an impostor who, while he affects to wear chains, is placed above those who are free; a chartered libertine that pretends to be manacled only that he may the more safely pick our pockets and lord it over our rights. This is the enemy we are now to encounter and overcome before we can expect to enjoy the substantial realities of freedom.

— Reading No. 26 —

ANDREW JACKSON: THE DANGER OF A MONEY MONOPOLY, 1837[26]

Jackson's long and successful war on The Monster is too familiar to permit rehearsal here. It is interesting to note that he did not think his crusade successful merely with the triumph over the Second Bank of the United States; it was still true, as he said in his Farewell Address, that "the agricultural, the mechanical, and the laboring classes have little or no share in the direction of the great moneyed corporations"; and it was still true that "the paper money system and its natural associates—monopoly and exclusive privileges" lingered on. We give

[26] From Andrew Jackson, Farewell Address, 1837, in Richardson, *Messages and Addresses of the Presidents,* II.

here Jackson's admonition to the American people on the dangers of a money monopoly.

ᛁ   ᛁ   ᛁ

It is one of the serious evils of our present system of banking that it enables one class of society, and that by no means a numerous one, by its control over the currency to act injuriously upon the interests of all the others and to exercise more than its just proportion of influence in political affairs. The agricultural, the mechanical, and the laboring classes have little or no share in the direction of the great moneyed corporations; and from their habits and the nature of their pursuits, they are incapable of forming extensive combinations to act together with united force. Such concert of action may sometimes be produced in a single city or in a small district of country by means of personal communications with each other; but they have no regular or active correspondence with those who are engaged in similar pursuits in distant places; they have but little patronage to give to the press and exercise but a small share of influence over it; they have no crowd of dependents above them who hope to grow rich without labor by their countenance and favor and who are, therefore, always ready to exercise their wishes. The planter, the farmer, the mechanic, and the laborer all know that their success depends upon their own industry and economy and that they must not expect to become suddenly rich by the fruits of their toil. Yet these classes of society form the great body of the people of the United States; they are the bone and sinew of the country; men who love liberty and desire nothing but equal rights and equal laws and who, moreover, hold the great mass of our national wealth, although it is distributed in moderate amounts among the millions of freemen who possess it. But, with overwhelming numbers and wealth on their side, they are in constant danger of losing their fair influence in the Government and with difficulty maintain their just rights against the incessant efforts daily made to encroach upon them. The mischief springs from the power which the moneyed interest derives from a paper currency which they are able to control; from the multitude of corporations with exclusive privileges which they have succeeded in obtaining in the different States and which are employed altogether for their benefit; and unless you become more watchful in your States and check this spirit of monopoly and thirst for exclusive privileges, you will, in the end, find that the most important powers of Government have been given or bartered away, and the control over your dearest interests has passed into the hands of these corporations.

The paper money system and its natural associates—monopoly and exclusive privileges—have already struck their roots deep in the soil; and it will require all your efforts to check its further growth and to eradicate the evil. The men who profit by the abuses and desire to perpetuate them will continue to besiege the halls of legislation in the General Government as well as in the States and will seek, by every artifice, to mislead and deceive the public servants. It is to yourselves that you must look for safety and the means of guarding and perpetuating your free institutions. In your hands is rightfully placed the sovereignty of the country and to you every one placed in authority is ultimately responsible. It is always in your power to see that the wishes of the people are carried into faithful execution, and their will, when once made known, must sooner or later be obeyed. And while the people remain, as I trust they ever will, uncorrupted and incorruptible and continue watchful and jealous of their rights, the Government is safe, and the cause of freedom will continue to triumph over all its enemies.

— Reading No. 27 —

THEODORE PARKER: THE BAD MERCHANT, 1846[27]

[27] From Theodore Parker, "A Sermon of Merchants," Nov. 22, 1846, in *Speeches, Addresses and Occasional Sermons* (Boston, 1852) I, 192 ff.

Better than any other reformer of his day with the
possible exception of Horace Greeley, the Reverend
Theodore Parker combined the two strains of Trans-
cendentalist idealism and secular practicality. He was
active not only in the assault on the orthodox churches,
or on the slaveocracy, or on behalf of the feeble and the
helpless, but in the attack on slums, on prostitution, on
the malpractices of banking and of industry, as well. We
give here an excerpt from his Sermon of Merchants, de-
livered in 1846.

✓   ✓   ✓

The wicked baron, bad of heart and bloody of hand,
has passed off with the ages which gave birth to such a
brood, but the bad merchant still lives. He cheats in his
trade; sometimes against the law, commonly with it. His
truth is never wholly true, nor his lie wholly false. He
overreaches the ignorant; makes hard bargains with men
in their trouble, for he knows that a falling man will
catch at red-hot iron. He takes the pound of flesh, though
that bring away all the life-blood with it. He loves private
contracts, digging through walls in secret. No interest is
illegal, if he can get it. He cheats the nation with false
invoices, and swears lies at the custom-house; will not
pay his taxes, but moves out of town on the last of April.
He oppresses the men who sail his ships, forcing them
to be temperate, only that he may consume the value of
their drink. He provides for them unsuitable bread and
meat. He would not engage in the African slave trade,
for he might lose his ships and perhaps more; but he is
always ready to engage in the American slave trade, and
calls you a "fanatic" if you tell him it is the worse of the
two. He cares not whether he sells cotton or the man who
wears it, if he only gets the money; cotton or negro, it
is the same to him. He would not keep a drink-hole in
Ann Street, only own and rent it. He will bring or make
whole cargoes of the poison that deals "damnation round
the land." He thinks it vulgar to carry rum about in a
jug, respectable in a ship. He makes paupers, and leaves
others to support them. Tell not him of the misery of
the poor, he knows better; nor of our paltry way of deal-
ing with public crime, he wants more jails and a speedier
gallows. You see his character in letting his houses, his

houses for the poor. He is a stone in the lame man's shoe. He is the poor man's devil. The Hebrew devil that so worried Job is gone; so is the brutal devil that awed our fathers. Nobody fears them; they vanish before cock-crowing. But this devil of the nineteenth century is still extant. He has gone into trade, and advertises in the papers; his name is "good" in the street. He "makes money;" the world is poorer by his wealth. He spends it as he made it, like a devil, on himself, his family alone, or worse yet, for show. He can build a church out of his gains, to have his morality, his Christianity preached in it, and call that the gospel, as Aaron called a calf— God. He sends rum and missionaries to the same bar-barians, the one to damn, the other to "save," both for his own advantage, for his patron saint is Judas, the first saint who made money out of Christ. Ask not him to do a good deed in private, "men would not know it," and "the example would be lost;" so he never lets a dollar slip out between his thumb and finger without leaving his mark on both sides of it. He is not forecast-ing to discern effects in causes, nor skilful to create new wealth, only spry in the scramble for what others have made. It is easy to make a bargain with him, hard to settle. In politics he wants a Government that will insure his dividends; so asks what is good for him, but ill for the rest. He knows no right, only power; no man but self; no God but his calf of gold.

What effect has he on young men? They had better touch poison. If he takes you to his heart, he takes you in. What influence on society? To taint and corrupt it all round. He contaminates trade; corrupt politics, mak-ing abusive laws, not asking for justice but only dividends. To the church he is the Anti-Christ. Yes the very Devil, and frightens the poor minister into shameful silence, or more shameless yet, into an apology for crime; makes him pardon the theory of crime! Let us look on that monster—look and pass by, not without prayer.

CHILD LABOR IN MASSACHUSETTS, 1825 [28]

During the colonial and early national periods, even very young children had done chores about the house or worked in the fields, and it was natural enough that the practice of child labor should be transferred from the farm to the factory. The conditions of child labor set forth in this report of a Committee on Education could be duplicated in every northern industrial state. Thus, of Pennsylvania it was said that "the principal part of the helps in cotton factories consist of boys and girls, we may safely say from six to seventeen years of age, (who) are confined to steady employment during the longest days in the year from daylight until dark. . . . It is entirely impossible for the parents of such children to obtain for them any education, save that of working the machine which they are compelled to work." In 1832 a Committee of the New England Association of Farmers, Mechanics and Workingmen reported that two-fifths of all operators in cotton mills were under 16 years of age, and that they customarily worked from 13 to 14 hours a day! In 1836 Massachusetts required a minimum of three months of schooling for all children under fourteen; not until 1842 did Massachusetts—the most advanced state in the Union in these matters—limit the labor of children in manufacturing to ten hours—and then only for children under twelve!

[28] From Report on Returns of Children Employed in Factories, Commonwealth of Massachusetts, 1825, in John R. Commons, *et al.*, eds. *Documentary History of American Industrial Society*, V, 60-61.

ABTRACT OF RETURNS OF CHILDREN EMPLOYED
IN MANUFACTORIES

	BOYS	GIRLS	
Amesbury	3	8	They attend school the principal part of the time at the Town School for 4 months
Brimfield	5	10	Work 12 hours each day—There is a good school at which they can attend as their parents judge proper
Boylston (West)	3	7	Work 12 hours p^r day. At school 8 weeks
Bellingham	11	9	Work 12 hours p^r day. No opp^y for School except by employ^g substitutes
Boston	14	0	No School^g
Bridgewater North	5	7	Work 12 hours. Cannot attend School & be employed
Cambridge	25	0	Can attend Eve^g school at the expence of the Manufact. Co.
Chelmsford	3	51	Work 12 hours
Danvers	0	1	Work 12 hours
Duxboro	1	10	Work from sunrise to sunset
Dorchester	8	30	Instruction well attended to
Franklin	4	2	Work 12 hours. Sunday School
Framingham	7	10	Work 12 hours. Are allowed 3 months for schooling
Hopkinton	6	4	Work 12 hours
Lancaster	0	4	Attend S. in winter
Leicester	5	5	Have 8 weeks Schooling
Ludlow	4	24	11 Hours work. Good village School
Marshfield	0	6	Work 6 months & attend School the rest of the time
Methuen	4	10	Some little chance for Sch^g
Newbury	4	2	Work 11 hours p^r day
Northboro	4	1	Work 11½ hours have attended S. very little. Propose to do better!
Pembroke	2	3	Work 12 hours
Rehoboth	8	13	Work 12 hours except in one factory for 2 mo. when there is no water
Southbridge	13	11	Average 12 hours—These children are better off than their neighbors!

Southbridge	7	9	Average 12 hours
"	2	1	" " "
"	7	5	" " "
Springfield	8	14	Work 12½ hours
Seekonk	59	80	Work 12 hours. Some may get 2 mo. school[g]
Troy*	34	69	Work all day. There are good public & private S. & a free Sunday School
Taunton	29	61	Work 12 hours—Sunday School
Waltham	17	59	As much opp[y] for School[g] as can be expected
Ware	4	9	Generally employ adults
Walpole	6	1	Work 9 mo.
Western	0	3	Work 8 mo.
Wellington	42	45	All day
	354	574	[sic 584] 928 TOTAL

* This town is now Fall River.

— Reading No. 29 —

THE CASE OF THE JOURNEYMAN TAILORS, 1836 [29]

Under the common-law doctrines that were accepted generally by American state courts, any combination of working men for the purpose of regulating the terms of employment or raising wages was a conspiracy in restraint of trade. Needless to say the same principle was not applied to combinations of bankers or businessmen, at this time. As American labor did not organize politically (the workingmen's parties were short-lived and ineffective) it had to win benefits through collective bar-

[29] From New York v. Faulkner, (1836) in John R. Commons, et al., eds., *Documentary History of American Industrial Society*, IV, 327 ff.

gaining; if bargaining was illegal, labor's position was desperate. In the 1830's a series of decisions held that labor organizations were, in fact, conspiracies. One of the most notorious of these was the decision in New York v. Faulkner involving a strike of New York City tailors. We give here an excerpt from Judge Edwards' opinion in that case.

✔   ✔   ✔

The Judge proceeded to pass sentence, which was done in the following words:

You have been convicted of a conspiracy. The bill of indictment charges substantially that you and others, being journeymen tailors, did perniciously form and unite yourselves into an unlawful club or combination to injure trade, and did make certain arbitrary by-laws, rules and orders, intending to govern not only yourselves but other journeymen tailors, and persons engaged in the business of tailors, and to oppress and injure them, and to injure trade and commerce. And also to prevent any journeymen tailors from working for any tailor who would not assent to said by-laws, that the said by-laws were to the effect following, viz. That you would not work for any tailor who would employ a journeyman tailor who was not a member of the said combination, or who would refuse to keep a slate hanging up in a public part of his store or shop, on which should be entered the name of every journeyman taking a job from his store, and that no journeyman should take one out of his turn. And also that no member of the said confederacy should go to any such shop for the purpose of getting a job, unless in his turn, under the penalty of forfeiting the price of the job. And also that no member should work for less than the bill of prices established by the club; nor for any tailor who employed a person who worked at a less price than the said bill of prices.

Also that during the period when there should be a strike, or turn out among such club, that a certain number of it should daily watch the shops of the persons against whom such strike or turn out was made, and that the person so appointed should serve, under the penalty of five dollars.

The indictment also charges, that you did, in presence

of such combination, refuse to work, and did in a violent and tumultuous manner assemble together, and did go about from place to place, and to the workshops of certain tailors, with the intent to alarm and terrify them and with the intent to persuade and deter other journeymen to leave and desist from their work, and did compel divers journeymen tailors to quit their employment.

Combining to do an act injurious to trade, is declared by a statute of this State, to be a misdemeanor.

That an offence, of the description of the one with which you are charged, is one within the act, has been unanimously decided by the Superior Court of this State, and for reasons which are deemed by the Court perfectly satisfactory. That such combinations are injurious to trade, has been fully verified in this city. Various trades have from time to time been brought to a stand, and the community extensively inconvenienced and embarrassed by them. The Legislature of this State, in conformity to the established principle of common law, in their wisdom thought it expedient that a remedy should be provided to the evil. They have, therefore, re-enacted the common law upon the subject with the additional provision, that some act shall be done to effect the object of it by one or more of the parties, in order to render it a misdemeanor.

The law leaves every individual master of his own individual acts. But it will not suffer him to encroach upon the rights of others. He may work or not, as suits his pleasure, but he shall not enter into a confederacy with a view of controlling others, and take measures to carry it into effect. The reason for the distinction is manifest. So long as individual members of the community do not resort to any acts of violence, their hostility can be guarded against. But who can withstand an extensive combination to injure him in his calling? When such cases, therefore, occur, the law extends its protecting shield.

Your case affords a striking manifestation of the necessity of the law extending its protection to the individual aimed at. The object of your combination was not only to control the merchant tailors, but even the journeymen. Your rules were craftily devised to accomplish this object, by throwing out of employment any master or journeyman who would not submit to your dictation.

But you were not content to stop here. You appointed committees to act as spies upon those whom you wished to subject to your will. Their premises were placed, day and night, under their vigilant inspection. You thronged around their shops, and were guilty of gross acts of indecorum. The journeymen who took jobs, were followed to their dwellings, and otherwise annoyed by you. In short, every ingenious device was resorted to by this extensive combination to which you were attached, to effect your object. Your conduct became insupportable, and the individuals aggrieved have found it necessary to appeal to the laws for protection; and a jury of your country has pronounced you guilty.

Associations of this description are of recent origin in this country. Here, where the government is purely paternal, where the people are governed by laws of their own creating; where the legislature proceeds with a watchful regard to the welfare not only of the whole, but of every class of society; where the representatives even lend a listening ear to the complaints of their constituents, it has not been found necessary or proper to subject any portion of the people to the control of self-created societies. Judging from what we have witnessed within the last year, we should be led to the conclusion that the trades of the country, which contribute immeasurably to its wealth, and upon which the prosperity of a most valuable portion of the community hinges, is rapidly passing from the control of the supreme power of the state into the hands of private societies. A state of things which would be as prejudicial in its consequences to the journeymen as it is to the employers, and all who have occasion for the fruits of their labor. In this favored land of law and liberty, the road to advancement is open to all, and the journeymen may be their skill and industry, and moral worth, soon become flourishing master mechanics. Combinations, which operate to the injury of the employers or of the trade, will in the regular course of events be found injurious to journeymen. Our trades and tradesmen have heretofore flourished without any such aid. Every American knows, or ought to know, that

108 THE ERA OF REFORM

he has no better friend than the laws, and that he needs
no artificial combination for his protection. Our experience never manifested their necessity, and I may confidently say that they were not the offspring of necessity.
They are of foreign origin, and I am led to believe are
mainly upheld by foreigners. If such is the fact, I would
say to them, that they mistake the character of the American people, if they indulge a hope that they can accomplish their ends in that way. No matter how crafty may
be their devices, nor how extensive may be their combinations, or violent may be their conduct, yet such is
the energy of the law, and such the fidelity of the people
to the government, that they will soon find their efforts
as unavailing as the beating of frothy surges against a
rock. It is a sentiment deeply engrafted in the bosom of
every American, that he ought and must submit to the
laws, and that to its mandates all stubborn necks must
yield.

Self-created societies are unknown to the constitution
and laws, and will not be permitted to rear their crest and
extend their baneful influence over any portion of the
community.

In fixing your punishment, we have duly considered
the recommendation of the jury, for we are under an
impression that you acted in ignorance of the law, and
we the more incline to this opinion, as we understand
that you are almost all foreigners. We have taken also
your poverty into consideration. But we admonish you,
and all others, that an ignorance of the law can no longer
be plead; that we shall consider future offenders as bold
defiers of the law, and treat them accordingly. The peace
of this community shall be no longer disturbed, and the
rights of individuals, and the interests of trade, sported
with as they have been, with impunity. The extensiveness
of the combinations, so far from insuring impunity, will
merit and will secure to the conspirators corresponding
punishment.

We have had in this country so little experience of
these combinations, that we are at a loss to know what
degree of severity may be necessary to rid society of
them. From the considerations which I have before
stated, and from a hope that the explicit declarations of
the law, not only by this, but by the Supreme Court,

will have the effect to prevent such practices, we are disposed to impose a very mild punishment, compared to the offence. But if this is not found to answer the purpose, we shall proceed from one degree of severity until the will of the people is obeyed; until the laws are submitted to.

Henry Faulkner, who was President of the society, shall be fined $150; Howell Vail, who made himself particularly conspicuous, $100—all other $50 each; and stand committed until the fine is paid.

— Reading No. 30 —

JUSTICE SHAW LEGALIZES UNIONS AND COLLECTIVE BARGAINING, 1842 [30]

The doctrine of such cases as New York v. Faulkner, and People v. Fisher would have made it impossible for labor to organize and to bargain collectively. Clearly it was necessary to repudiate the common-law doctrine of conspiracy embedded in these decisions. This was achieved in the notable case of Commonwealth v. Hunt, in Massachusetts, and remarkably enough it was the conservative Chief Justice Lemuel Shaw who was responsible for the triumph of the more enlightened point of view.

✓   ✓   ✓

This was an indictment against the defendants (seven in number), for a conspiracy. The first count alleged that the defendants, together with divers other persons unknown to the grand jurors, "on the first Monday of Sep-

[30] From Commonwealth v. Hunt, 4 Metcalf 45, Mass. Reports (1842).

tember 1840, at Boston, being workmen and journeymen
in the art and manual occupation of boot-makers, unlawfully, perniciously and deceitfully designing and intending to continue, keep up, form, and unite themselves
into an unlawful club, society and combination . . . did
unlawfully assemble and meet together, and . . . did
then and there unjustly and corruptly . . . agree together, that none of them would work for any master
or person whatsoever, in the said art, mystery or occupation, who should employ any workman or journeyman,
or other person, in the said art, who was not a member
of said club, society or combination, after notice given
him to discharge such workman from the employ of such
master; to the great damage and oppression, not only of
their said masters employing them in said art and occupation, but also of divers other workmen and journeymen in the said art, mystery and occupation; to the evil
example of all others in like case offending, and against
the peace and dignity of the Commonwealth."

The second count charged that the defendants, and
others unknown, at the time and place mentioned in the
first count, "did unlawfully assemble, meet, conspire, confederate and agree together, not to work for any master
or person who should employ any workman not being a
member of a club, society or combination, called the
Boston Journeymen Bootmakers' Society in Boston, in
Massachusetts, or should break any of their by-laws, unless such workman should pay to said club and society
such sum as should be agreed upon as a penalty for the
breach of such unlawful rules, orders and by-laws; and
by means of said conspiracy, they did compel one Isaac
B. Wait, a master cordwainer in said Boston, to turn out
of his employ one Jeremiah Horne, a journeyman boot-
maker, because said Horne would not pay a sum of
money to said society for an alleged penalty of some of
said unjust rules, orders and by-laws." . . .

The defendants were found guilty, at the October term,
1840, of the municipal court, and thereupon several exceptions were alleged by them to the ruling of the judge
at the trial. The only exception, which was considered in
this court, was this: "The defendants' counsel contended
that the indictment did not set forth any agreement to do
a criminal act, or to do any lawful act by criminal means;

and that the agreements, therein set forth, did not constitute a conspiracy indictable by any law of this Commonwealth; and they moved the court so to instruct the jury: But the judge refused so to do, and instructed the jury that the indictment against the defendants did, in his opinion, describe a confederacy among the defendants to do an unlawful act, and to effect the same by unlawful means: That the society, organized and associated for the purpose described in the indictment, was an unlawful conspiracy, against the laws of this Commonwealth. . . .

SHAW, C. J. . . . We have no doubt, that by the operation of the constitution of this Commonwealth, the general rules of the common law, making conspiracy an indictable offence, are in force here, and that this is included in the description of laws which had, before the adoption of the constitution, been used and approved in the Province, Colony, or State of Massachusetts Bay, and usually practised in the courts of law. . . . Still it is proper in this connexion to remark, that although the common law in regard to conspiracy in this Commonwealth is in force, yet it will not necessarily follow that every indictment at common law for this offence is a precedent for a similar indictment in this State. The general rule of the common law is, that it is a criminal and indictable offence, for two or more to confederate and combine together, by concerted means, to do that which is unlawful or criminal, to the injury of the public, or portions or classes of the community, or even to the rights of an individual. This rule of law may be equally in force as a rule of the common law, in England and in this Commonwealth; and yet it must depend upon the local laws of each country to determine, whether the purpose to be accomplished by the combination, or the concerted means of accomplishing it, be unlawful or criminal in the respective countries. All those laws of the parent country, whether rules of the common law, or early English statutes, which were made for the purpose of regulating the wages of laborers, the settlement of paupers, and making it penal for anyone to use a trade or handicraft to which he had not served a full apprenticeship—not being adapted to the circumstances of our colonial condition—were not adopted, used or approved, and therefore do not come within the description of the

laws adopted and confirmed by the provision of the constitution already cited. . . .

Stripped then of these introductory recitals and alleged
injurious consequences, and of the qualifying epithets
attached to the facts, the averment is this; that the defendants and others formed themselves into a society,
and agreed not to work for any person who should employ any journeyman or other person, not a member of
such society, after notice given him to discharge such
workman. The manifest intent of the association is, to
induce all those engaged in the same occupation to become members of it. Such a purpose is not unlawful. It
would give them a power which might be exerted for
useful and honorable purposes, or for dangerous and
pernicious ones. If the latter were the real and actual
object, and susceptible of proof, it should have been
specially charged. Such an association might be used to
afford each other assistance in times of poverty, sickness
and distress; or to raise their intellectual, moral and social condition; or to make improvement in their art; or
for other proper purposes. Or the association might be
designed for purposes of oppression and injustice. . . .

Nor can we perceive that the objects of this association, whatever they may have been, were to be attained
by criminal means. The means which they proposed to
employ, as averred in this count, and which, as we are
now to presume, were established by the proof, were,
that they would not work for a person, who, after due
notice, should employ a journeyman not a member of
their society. Supposing the object of the association to
be laudable and lawful, or at least not unlawful, are these
means criminal? The case supposes that these persons are
not bound by contract, but free to work for whom they
please, or not to work, if they so prefer. In this state of
things, we cannot perceive, that it is criminal for men to
agree together to exercise their own acknowledged rights,
in such a maner as best to subserve their own interests.
One way to test this is, to consider the effect of such an
agreement, where the object of the association is acknowledged on all hands to be a laudable one. Suppose a
class of workmen, impressed with the manifold evils on
intemperance, should agree with each other not to work
in a shop in which ardent spirit was furnished, or not

to work in a shop with any one who used it, or not to work for an employer, who should, after notice, employ a journeyman who habitually used it. The consequences might be the same. A workman, who should still persist in the use of ardent spirit, would find it more difficult to get employment; a master employing such an one might, at times, experience inconvenience in his work, in losing the services of a skilful but intemperate workman. Still it seems to us, that as the object would be lawful, and the means not unlawful, such an agreement could not be pronounced a criminal conspiracy. . . .

We think, therefore, that associations may be entered into, the object of which is to adopt measures that may have a tendency to impoverish another, that is, to diminish his gains and profits, and yet so far from being criminal or unlawful, the object may be highly meritorious and public spirited. The legality of such an association will therefore depend upon the means to be used for its accomplishment. . . .

VI

LAND REFORM

— Reading No. 31 —

FEUDAL TENURE IN NEW YORK AND THE ANTIRENT TROUBLES, 1844-46 [31]

[31] From (a) Report of Committee of the State of New York, Documents of the Assembly, 67th Sess. 1844, Vol. VII, Doc. no. 189. (b) Report of the Debates and Proceedings of the Convention for the Revision of the Constitution . . . (Albany 1846) 1051-2.

*Vast patroonships—or manors—survived in New York
from colonial days well into the 19th century: that of
Rensselaerwyck on the upper Hudson, for example, embraced an area twenty-four by forty-eight miles. The pa-
troons would not alienate their lands, but rented them
out on long, or perpetual, leases at a nominal rent.
They did, however, exact feudal dues, notably a charge
of one-fourth of the sale price on each piece of land that
changed hands. Stephen Van Rensselaer, "the good pa-
troon" had not been too exacting with his tenants; the
attempt of his heirs to collect back debts and to enforce
ancient prerogatives led to widespread discontent, riots,
and violence. This was the famous Rent War which furnished material for Cooper's vitriolic novels,* The Chain-
bearer *and* The Redskins. *Even though a legislative committee had deplored the remnants of feudalism and vindicated the position of the tenants, Governor Silas Wright
put down the antirenters with a firm, if not a heavy hand.
The framers of the new constitution of 1846, however,
confessed the validity of the antirent program by writing
into the constitution the abolition of feudal tenures, and
prohibiting any leases for more than twelve years. And
the new Governor John Young pardoned the antirenters
imprisoned for their participation in the rent war.*

*We give here two documents: first a report of a leg-
islative committee on feudal tenure in New York, and
second, part of the debate on the abolition of feudal
tenures in the Constitutional Convention of 1846.*

✓   ✓   ✓

(a) Report on Feudal Tenures in New York

. . . Your committee are of the opinion that the conditions, and especially the reservations in these leases, are
extremely onerous to the tenants; that they have a direct
tendency to suppress that spirit of enterprise and improvement so essential to promote the prosperity of this country; and that they are in many respects repugnant to the
genius of our republican institutions. These leases had
their origin in Europe in the age of feudalism, and still
preserve those restrictions which were engrafted upon
them at that barbarous period, and which are so justly
odious to every friend of free institutions of government.

These restrictions were devised by the sovereigns and

nobles of the several nations of Europe, for the express purpose of strengthening their own power and increasing their own wealth, while at the same time they weakened and impoverished their unhappy tenants. Their sole object was to convert their tenants into abject serfs or slaves, and make them mere appendages of the soil, and to be kept forever in a condition of hopeless vassalage, without a prospect of relief. . . .

The American people are emphatically an emigrating people. From almost every township in the older States, large colonies of farmers and mechanics have emigrated to new settlements in the west. But many of the tenants of the manor of Rensselaerwyck are unable to avail themselves, without great sacrifice, of the privilege enjoyed by their fellow citizens in other sections of the Union. If they wish to dispose of their property, one quarter of its price is liable to be forfeited to the proprietor of the manor. A restriction of this nature your committee feel confident, must be regarded as extremely unjust and oppressive, and as operating most effectually to check if not to arrest altogether the prosperity of that community in which it is in force. In many countries of Europe, this, as well as other barbarous features of the feudal system, have long since been abolished by express laws; shall it be suffered to remain longer as a reproach to the intelligence and civilization of a free republic? The reservation by the lessors of the manor of all water privileges, your committee regard as in the highest degree injurious to the improvement and prosperity of the two counties in which the manor is situated. . . .

Such a condition of things, the House will not fail to perceive, must be productive of serious and lasting injury to the interests of the inhabitants of the manor. While other sections of the State, untrammeled by any particle of these oppressions and anti republican restrictions which exist in the manor of Rensselaerwyck, are advancing with giant strides in all the elements of moral and physical greatness, the inhabitants of this manor are condemned, by the hard tenure of the leases which their honest and unsuspecting ancestors bequeathed them, to toil on from year to year, in a condition of comparative servitude, depressed by a constant blight upon their prosperity, and unrelieved by the prospect of a release from their burthens. . . .

In fine, your committee believe that the conditions and reservations of these leases are of such a nature as to obstruct trade, by fettering the transfer of property with oppressive restrictions, injurious to those who are compelled to submit to them; that they tend in a very material degree to discourage that spirit of improvement so indispensable to the growth of every community, and by depriving the tenants of that feeling of independence, which should always characterise the freemen, to lower them in the intellectual scale, to depress and weaken their moral energies, and assimilate them, in a painful degree, to the unfortunate beings who toil and groan through a miserable existence under the feudal despotisms of the old world. . . .

(b) Debate in the Constitutional Convention

1. All feudal tenures of every description, with all their incidents are abolished.

2. No lease or grant of agricultural land for a longer period than ten years, hereafter made, in which shall be reserved any rent or service of any kind, shall be valid.

3. All covenants or conditions in any grant of land whereby the right of the grantee to alien is in any manner restrained, and all fines, quarter sales, and other charges upon alienation reserved, in every grant of land hereafter to be made, shall be void.

MR. JORDAN said there was a just feeling against the occupancy of farms belonging to a lord who exercised the same rights over his tenants as a lord in England, and holds on to his lands merely from the pride of being the lord over the manor. These were rights reserved to the owners after the revolution because it was private property. But they were inconsistent with the spirit of our republican institutions, and should be abolished. It was not proper to give the cold shoulder to these tenants and tell them to go about their business, because their requests were mere folly; they had these feudal tenures already abolished, and we had no fear that the legislature would ever revive them. He wished it to be placed in the constitution beyond the power of the legislature to touch it. It would have some effect to allay that natural spirit of oppugnation to the idea of living upon a farm held under these tenures, whose owner has a right to say 'you owe

me a day's riding, and you must pay it,' not because he
has any need of the service, but because he has some
pride in displaying his authority, and some pride in having it to say, 'I am the lord of this broad domain!' We wish
to have these tenures and their incidents abolished, and
constitutionally abolished. He would not have a man
released from paying his rent when he legally owed it,
unless he could get released from it in a lawful way. The
payment of rent was not what was complained of. He
gave some instances of the terms of leases in which the
tenant was obliged to get permission in writing if he
entertained a stranger in his house for twenty-four hours;
that he should trade in nothing else than the produce of
the manor; that he should trade at the store and grind his
flour at the mill of the proprietor, &c., &c. It was from
such things that relief was asked; which, although the
moral sense of the community will not admit to be
enforced, are still actually in existence.

— Reading No. 32 —

PRE-EMPTION ACT OF 1841 [32]

*Individual settlers, pushing ahead of government sur-
veys, squatted on the public domain, and, not unnaturally,
thought it a grave injustice when lands which they had
cleared, cultivated, and improved, were put up for public
sale. Actually, Congress had made special provision for
many squatters on public lands in the past, but not until
1841 did it get around to enacting a general pre-emption
law.*

[32] From U. S. Statutes at Large, V, 453 ff, in Commager,
Documents of American History, Doc. no. 157.

✔   ✔   ✔

An Act to appropriate the proceeds of the sales of public lands and to grant pre-emption rights.

Sec. 8. That there shall be granted to each State . . . five hundred thousand acres of land for . . . internal improvements. *Provided,* that to each of the States which has already received grants for said purposes, there is hereby granted no more than a quantity of land which shall, together with the amount said State has already received . . . make five hundred thousand acres. . . .

Sec. 9. . . . That the net proceeds of the sale of said lands shall be faithfully applied to objects of internal improvement . . . namely, roads, railways, bridges, canals and improvement of water-courses, and draining of swamps. . . .

Sec. 10. That from and after the passage of this act, every . . . man, over the age of twenty-one years, and being a citizen of the United States, or having filed his declaration of intention to become a citizen . . . who since the first day of June, A. D. eighteen hundred and forty, has made . . . a settlement in person on the public lands to which the Indian title had been . . . extinguished, and which . . . shall have been surveyed prior thereto, and who shall inhabit and improve the same, and who . . . shall erect a dwelling thereon, . . . is hereby, authorized to enter with . . . the land office . . . by legal subdivisions, any number of acres not exceeding one hundred and sixty, or a quarter section of land, to include the residence of such claimant, upon paying to the United States the minimum price of such land, subject, however, to the following limitations and exceptions: No person shall be entitled to more than one pre-emptive right by virtue of this act; no person who is the proprietor of three hundred and twenty acres of land in any State or Territory of the United States, and no person who shall quit or abandon his residence on his own land to reside on the public land in the same State or Territory, shall acquire any right of pre-emption under this act; no lands included in any reservation . . . no lands reserved for the support of schools, nor the lands . . . to which the title has been or may be extinguished by the United States at any time during the operation of this act; no section of land reserved to the United States alternate to other sections granted to any of the States for the construction of any canal, railroad, or other . . . public improvement; no sections . . . included within the limits of any incorporated town; no portions of the public lands which have been selected as the site for a city or town; no parcel or lot of land actually settled and occupied for the purposes of trade and not agriculture; and no lands on which are situated any known salines or mines, shall be liable to entry under and by virtue of the provisions of this act. . . .

Sec. 11. That when two or more persons shall have settled on the same quarter section of land, the right of pre-emption shall be in him or her who made the first settlement, provided such persons shall conform to the other provisions of this act; and all questions as to the right of pre-emptions arising between different settlers shall be settled by the register and receiver of the district within which the land is situated, subject to an appeal to and a revision by the Secretary of the Treasury of the United States. . . .

— Reading No. 33 —

GEORGE HENRY EVANS AND THE BEGINNINGS OF HOMESTEAD AGITATION, 1844 [33]

[33] From the *Working Man's Advocate*, 30 Nov. 1844, in John R. Commons, *et al.*, eds., *Documentary History of American Industrial Society*, VII, 317 ff.

From the very beginning there was a conflict between those who wished to hold public lands for revenue, and those who believed that they should be thrown open to settlers free. The official policy was to sell public lands at a fairly high price; the pressure of public opinion brought the price down, made terms of sale easier, and—as we have seen—permitted actual settlers to pre-empt the land they had farmed and improved. As early as 1825 Thomas Hart Benton urged that public lands be given to settlers; by the late 'thirties and 'forties this policy commanded widespread support, and by 1848 became one of the important planks in the platform of the Free Soil Party. The first major agitator for a homestead policy was the English-born George Henry Evans. Deeply influenced by Thomas Paine, Evans devoted his life to championing the welfare of the workingmen of America. With the collapse of the workers' movements during the depression of 1837 Evans retired to his farm in New Jersey and devoted himself to study; he emerged in 1844 to edit the Working Man's Advocate *and agitate a homestead policy. Perhaps his most important contribution was in winning the enthusiastic support of Horace Greeley to this cause. We give here a memorial from "citizens of New York," doubtlessly written by the indefatigable Evans.*

✔   ✔   ✔

MEMORIAL TO CONGRESS

The undersigned Citizens of New York respectfully represent that, in their opinion, the system of Land Traffic imported to this country from Europe is wrong in principle; that it is fast debasing us to the condition of a nation of dependant tenants, of which condition a rapid increase of inequality, misery, pauperism, vice, and crime are the necessary consequences; and that, therefore now, in the infancy of the Republic, we should take effectual measures to eradicate the evil, and establish a principle more in accordance with our republican theory, as laid down in the Declaration of Independence; to which end we propose that the General Government shall no longer traffic, or permit traffic, in the Public Lands yet in its possession, and that they shall be laid out in Farms and Lots for the free use of such citizens (not possessed of other land) as will occupy them, allowing the settler the right to dispose of his possession to any one not possessed of other land; and that the jurisdiction of the Public Lands be transferred to States only on condition that such a disposition should be made of them.

Your memorialists offer the following reasons for such a disposition of the lands as they propose:

1. It would increase the number of freeholders and decrease the anti-republican dependence of those who might not become freeholders; exactly reversing the state of things now in progress.

2. As the drain of the population would gradually be to where the land was free, the price of all land held for traffic would gradually decrease, till, ultimately, the land-holders would see greater advantages in an Agrarian plan that would make every man a freeholder, than in the system of land-selling, under which their children might become dependent tenants.

3. City populations would diminish gradually till every inhabitant could be the owner of a comfortable habitation; and the country population would be more compactly settled, making less roads and bridges necessary, and giving greater facilities of education.

4. There need be no Standing Army, for there would soon be a chain of Townships along the frontiers, settled by independent freemen, willing and able to protect the country.

5. The danger of Indian aggressions would be materially lessened if our people only took possession of land enough for their use.

6. The strongest motive to encroachments by Whites on the rights of the Indians would be done away with by prohibiting speculation in land.

7. The ambition, avarice, or enterprise that would, under the present system, add acre to acre, would be directed, more usefully, to the improvement of those to which each man's possession was limited.

8. There would be no Repudiation of State Debts, for, let people settle the land compactly, and they could, and would, make all desirable improvements without going into debt.

9. National prosperity and the prosperity of the masses would be coincident, here again reversing the present order of things, of which England is a notable example.

10. Great facilities would be afforded to test the various plans of Association, which now engage the attention of so large a proportion of our citizens, and which have been found to work so well, so far as the accumulation of wealth and the prevention of crime and pauperism are concerned, in the case of those longest established, for instance, the Zoarites, Rappites, and Shakers.

11. The now increasing evil of office-seeking would be diminished, both by doing away with the necessity of many offices now in existence, and by enabling men to obtain a comfortable existence without degrading themselves to become office beggars. Cincinnatus and Washington could with difficulty be prevailed upon to take office, because they knew there was more real enjoyment in the cultivation of their own homesteads.

12. It would, in a great measure, do away the now necessary evil of laws and lawyers, as there could be no disputes about rents, mortgages, or land titles, and morality would be promoted by the encouragement and protection of industry.

13. As the people of England are now fast turning their attention to the recovery of their long-lost right to the soil, it would give them encouragement in their object, and enable them the sooner to furnish happy homes for the thousands who otherwise would come among us as exiles from their native land.

14. The principle of an Equal Right to the Soil once established, would be the recognition of a truth that has been lost sight of by civilization, and which, in our opinion, would tend powerfully to realize the glorious aspirations of philanthropists, universal peace and universal freedom.

New York, 1844.

— Reading No. 34 —

"VOTE YOURSELF A FARM," 1846[34]

This appeal, which first appeared in the True Workingman, *January 24, 1846, was distributed as a handbill by
the thousands. Probably written by Evans, the phrase
"Vote Yourself a Farm" was taken up by Greeley and,
later on, by the Free Soil party.*

↗   ↗   ↗

Are you an American citizen? Then you are a joint-
owner of the public lands. Why not take enough of
your property to provide yourself a home? Why not
vote yourself a farm?

Remember poor Richard's saying: "Now I have a
sheep and a cow, every one bids me 'good morrow.'"
If a man have a house and a home of his own, though
it be a thousand miles off, he is well received in other
people's houses; while the homeless wretch is turned
away. The bare right to a farm, though you should
never go near it, would save you from many an insult.
Therefore, Vote yourself a farm.

Are you a party follower? Then you have long enough
employed your vote to benefit scheming office-seekers;
use it for once to benefit yourself—Vote yourself a farm.

Are you tired of slavery—of drudging for others—of
poverty and its attendant miseries? Then, Vote yourself
a farm.

Are you endowed with reason? Then you must know
that your right to life hereby includes the right to a
place to live in—the right to a home. Assert this right,
so long denied mankind by feudal robbers and their
attorneys. Vote yourself a farm.

[34] From *True Workingman,* Jan. 24, 1846, in J. R. Commons,
   et al., eds. *Documentary History of American Industrial
   Society,* VII, 305-7.

Are you a believer in the scriptures? Then assert that the land is the Lord's, because He made it. Resist then the blasphemers who exact money for His work, even as you would resist them should they claim to be worshipped for His holiness. Emancipate the poor from the necessity of encouraging such blasphemy—Vote the freedom of the public lands.

Are you a man? Then assert the sacred rights of man —especially your right to stand upon God's earth and to till it for your own profit. Vote yourself a farm.

Would you free your country, and the sons of toil everywhere, from the heartless, irresponsible mastery of the aristocracy of avarice? Would you disarm this aristocracy of its chief weapon, the fearful power of banishment from God's earth? Then join with your neighbors to form a true American party, having for its guidance the principles of the American revolution, and whose chief measures shall be—1. To limit the quantity of land that any one man may henceforth monopolize or inherit; and 2. To make the public lands free to actual settlers only, each having the right to sell his improvements to any man not possessed of other land. These great measures once carried, wealth would become a changed social element; it would then consist of the accumulated products of human labor, instead of a hoggish monoply of the products of God's labor; and the antagonism of capital and labor would forever cease. Capital could no longer grasp the largest share of the laborer's earnings, as a reward for not doing him all the injury the laws of the feudal aristocracy authorize, viz: the denial of all stock to work upon and all place to live in. To derive any profit from the laborer, it must first give him work; for it could no longer wax fat by levying a dead tax upon his existence. The hoary iniquities of Norman land pirates would cease to pass current as American law. Capital, with its power for good undiminished, would lose the power to oppress; and a new era would dawn upon the earth, and rejoice the souls of a thousand generations. Therefore forget not to Vote yourself a farm.

— Reading No. 35 —

THE HOMESTEAD ACT, 1860[35]

Beginning in the late 'forties Andrew Johnson, Horace Greeley, and others introduced some form of homestead bill into almost every session of Congress. On February 1, 1859, a liberal Homestead bill actually passed the lower House by a vote of 120-76, but was laid on the table in the Senate by the casting vote of Vice-President Breckinridge. The 1860 bill which we give here was sponsored by Mr. Owen Lovejoy of Illinois and Andrew Johnson of Tennessee; it passed both houses by overwhelming majorities, but was vetoed by President Buchanan on constitutional grounds. In May, 1862, with Democratic opposition weakened, the Republicans passed and President Lincoln signed a Homestead Act.

✔　　　✔　　　✔

AN ACT to secure homesteads to actual settlers on the public domain, and for other purposes.

Be it enacted. . . . , That any person who is the head of a family and a citizen of the United States shall, from and after the passage of this act, be entitled to enter one quarter section of vacant and unappropriated public lands . . . to be located in a body . . . after the same shall have been surveyed, upon the following conditions: That the person applying for the benefit of this act shall . . . make affidavit before the . . . register or receiver of said land office that he or she is the head of a family, and is actually settled on the quarter-section . . . proposed to be entered, and that such application is made for his or her use and benefit . . . and not either directly or indirectly for the use or benefit of any other person or persons whomsoever, and that he or she has never at

[35] From Thomas Donaldson, *The Public Domain* (Washington, 1884) 340.

any previous time had the benefit of this act; and upon making the affidavit as above required . . . he or she shall thereupon be permitted to enter the quantity of land already specified; *Provided however,* that no final certificate shall be given, or patent issued therefore, until the expiration of five years from the date of such entry; and if, at the expiration of such time, the person making such entry . . . shall prove by two credible witnesses, that he, she, or they—that is to say, some member or members of the same family—has or have erected a dwelling-house upon said land, and continued to reside upon and cultivate the same for the term of five years, and still reside upon the same (and that neither the said land nor any part thereof has been alienated); then, in such case, he, she, or they, upon the payment of 25 cents per acre for the quantity entered, shall be entitled to a patent. . . . *And provided further,* That all entries made under the provisions of this section, upon lands which have not been offered for public sale, shall be confined to and upon sections designated by odd numbers.

VII

EDUCATION

— Reading No. 36 —

THE MASSACHUSETTS HIGH SCHOOL ACT, 1827[36]

Though the Bay Colony had made provision for education as early as 1642 and had required each town to provide elementary education for the young in the famous

[36] From *Laws of Massachusetts, January Session, 1827,* ch. XCLIII, in E. W. Knight and C. L. Hall, *Readings in American Educational History* (New York, 1951) 247.

act of 1647, and had set up a college in 1636, it had made only the most casual provision for secondary education. For the most part secondary education was provided by the hundreds of academies that grew up in the late 18th and early 19th centuries. These were commonly denominational in character; charged tuition; and were open only to boys. The ferment of educational reform that swept the western world in the first quarter of the 19th century, was responsible for this first high school law of 1827, and for significant progress in secondary education generally throughout the North.

✟　　　✟　　　✟

Be it enacted, That each town or district within this Commonwealth, containing fifty families, or householders, shall be provided with a teacher or teachers, of good morals, to instruct children in orthography, reading, writing, English grammar, geography, arithmetic, and good behavior, for such term of time as shall be equivalent to six months for one school in each year; and every town or district containing one hundred families or householders, shall be provided with such teacher or teachers, for such term of time as shall be equivalent to eighteen months, for one school in each year. In every city, town, or district, containing five hundred families, or householders shall be provided with such teacher or teachers for such term of time as shall be equivalent to twenty-four months, shall also be provided with a master of good morals, competent to instruct, in addition to the branches of learning aforesaid, in the history of the United States, bookkeeping by single entry, geometry, surveying, algebra; and shall employ such master to instruct a school in such city, town, or district, for the benefit of all the inhabitants thereof, at least ten months in each year, exclusive of vacations, in such convenient places, or alternately at such places in such city, town, or district, as said inhabitants, at their meeting in March, or April, annually, shall determine; and in every city, or town, and district, containing four thousand inhabitants, such master shall be competent in addition to all the foregoing branches, to instruct the Latin and Greek languages, history, rhetoric, and logic.

— Reading No. 37 —

ABRAHAM LINCOLN ON THE VITAL IMPORTANCE OF EDUCATION, 1832 [37]

Shortly after Lincoln came to New Salem—he was just 23—he offered himself as a candidate for the General Assembly, and issued a "platform" in the form of a "Communication to the People of Sangamo County." He was defeated, but carried his own town of New Salem by a heavy majority. Lincoln's concern for education was by no means unusual on the American frontier; the schoolmaster went west with the pioneer, and within a few years Illinois would boast a handful of colleges.

✓   ✓   ✓

March 9, 1832

FELLOW-CITIZENS: Having become a candidate for the honorable office of one of your representatives in the next General Assembly of this state, in accordance with an established custom, and the principles of true republicanism, it becomes my duty to make known to you . . . my sentiments with regard to local affairs. . . .

Upon the subject of education, not presuming to dictate any plan or system respecting it, I can only say that I view it as the most important subject which we as a people can be engaged in. That every man may receive at least, a moderate education, and thereby be enabled to read the histories of his own and other countries, by which he may duly appreciate the value of our free institutions, appears to be an object of vital importance, even on this account alone, to say nothing of the ad-

---

[37] From Abraham Lincoln, "Communication to the People of Sangamo County" in *The Collected Works of Abraham Lincoln,* ed. by Roy P. Basler, *et al.* (New Brunswick, New Jersey, 1953) I, 5, 8.

vantages and satisfaction to be derived from being able to read the scriptures and other works, both of a religious and moral nature, for themselves. For my part, I desire to see the time when education, and by its means, morality, sobriety, enterprise, and industry, shall become much more general than at present, and should be gratified to have it in my power to contribute something to the advancement of any measure which might have a tendency to accelerate the happy period. . . .

— Reading No. 38 —

THADDEUS STEVENS: PLEA FOR PUBLIC EDUCATION IN PENNSYLVANIA, 1835 [38]

Thaddeus Stevens had been elected to the Pennsylvania legislature on an Anti-Masonic ticket in 1833. The following year he helped push through a bill extending the free public school system then flourishing in Philadelphia to the rest of the State. The cost of this public school system led to clamorous demands for the repeal of the bill; Stevens's eloquent plea for public education not only averted repeal but won him a nationwide reputation.

✦   ✦   ✦

It would seem to be humiliating to be under the necessity, in the nineteenth century, of entering into a formal argument, to prove the utility, and, to free governments, the absolute necessity of education. More than

[38] From Thaddeus Stevens, "Speech against the Repeal of the School Law," April 1835, in *Annual Report . . . of the Commissioner of Education for 1899* (Washington, 1900) I, 519 ff.

two thousand years ago the Deity who presided over intellectual endowments, ranked highest for dignity, chastity, and virtue among the goddesses worshipped by cultivated pagans. And I will not insult this house of our constituents by supposing any course of reasoning necessary to convince them of its high importance. Such necessity would be degrading to a Christian age, a free Republic.

If, then, education be of admitted importance to the people, under all forms of government, and of unquestioned necessity, when they govern themselves, it follows, of course, that its cultivation and diffusion is a matter of public concern, . . .

If an elective Republic is to endure for any great length of time, every elector must have sufficient information, not only to accumulate wealth and take care of his pecuniary concerns, but to direct wisely the legislature, the ambassadors, and the Executive of the nation—for some part of all these things, some agency in approving or disapproving of them, falls to every freeman. If, then, the permanency of our Government depends upon such knowledge, it is the duty of government to see that the means of information be diffused to every citizen. This is a sufficient answer to those who deem education a private and not a public duty—who argue that they are willing to educate their own children, but not their neighbors' children. . . .

This law is often objected to, because its benefits are shared by the children of the profligate spendthrift equally with those of the most industrious and economical habits. It ought to be remembered that the benefit is bestowed, not upon the erring parents, but the innocent children. Carry out this objection and you punish children for the crimes or misfortunes of their parents. You virtually establish cases and grades founded on no merit of the particular generation, but on the demerits of their ancestors; an aristocracy of the most odious and insolent kind—the aristocracy of wealth and pride.

It is said that its advantages will be unjustly and unequally enjoyed, because the industrious, money-making man keeps his whole family constantly employed, and has but little time for them to spend at school; while the idle man has but little employment for his family, and they will constantly attend school. I know, sir, that there are some men, whose whole souls are so completely absorbed in the accumulation of wealth, and whose avarice so increases with success, that they look upon their very children in no other light than as instruments of gain—that they, as well as the ox and the ass within their gates, are valuable only in proportion to their annual earnings. And, according to the present system, the children of such men are reduced almost to an intellectual level with their colaborers of the brute creation. This law will be of vast advantage to the offspring of such misers. If they are compelled to pay their taxes to support schools, their very meanness will induce them to send their children to them to get the worth of their money. Thus it will extract good out of the very penuriousness of the miser. Surely a system which will work such wonders, ought to be as greedily sought for, and more highly prized, than that coveted alchemy which was to produce gold and silver out of the blood and entrails of vipers, lizards, and other filthy vermin. . . .

In giving this law to posterity you act the part of the philanthropist, by bestowing upon the poor as well as the rich the greatest earthly boon which they are capable of receiving; you act ·the part of the philosopher by pointing if you do not lead them up the hill of science; you act the part of the hero if it be true as you say that popular vengeance follows close upon your footsteps. Here, then, if you wish true popularity, is a theater in which you may acquire it. What renders the name of Socrates immortal but his love of the human family exhibited under all circumstances and in contempt of every danger? But courage, even with but little benevolence may confer lasting renown. It is this which makes us bow with involuntary respect at the name of Napoleon, of Caesar, and of Richard of the Lion Heart. But what earthly glory is there equal in luster and duration to that conferred by education? What else could have bestowed such renown upon the philosophers, the poets, the statesmen, and orators of antiquity? What else could have conferred such undisputed applause upon Aristotle, Demosthenes, and Homer; on Virgil, Horace, and Cicero? And is learning less interesting and important now than it was in centuries past, when those statesmen and orators charmed and ruled empires with their eloquence?

— Reading No. 39 —

HORACE MANN ON EDUCATION AND NATIONAL WELFARE, 1848 [39]

Two great names dominate the history of the educational revival and reformation that swept the United States in the second quarter of the century: Horace Mann and Henry Barnard. Mann's appointment as the first Secretary of the newly created Board of Education of Massachusetts inaugurated an era in the history of America education. During the years he served in this position, Mann issued a series of twelve annual reports; these went far beyond the demands of the ordinary report to survey the needs, the methods, the potentialities of public education in America and in free societies generally. The twelfth, and final, report is particularly notable for its eloquent discussion of the relation of public education to national welfare.

✓   ✓   ✓

. . . . A cardinal object which the government of Massachusetts, and all the influential men in the State, should propose to themselves, is the physical well-being of all the people,—the sufficiency, comfort, competence, of every individual in regard to food, raiment, and shelter. And these necessaries and conveniences of life should be obtained by each individual for himself, or by each family for themselves, rather than accepted from the hand of charity or extorted by poor-laws. It is not averred that this most desirable result can, in all instances, be obtained;

[39] From Horace Mann, "Twelfth Annual Report . . . as Secretary of Massachusetts State Board of Education," in Commager, *Documents of American History*, Doc. No. 173.

but it is, nevertheless, the end to be aimed at. True states-
manship and true political economy, not less than true
philanthropy, present this perfect theory as the goal, to
be more and more closely approximated by our imperfect
practice. The desire to achieve such a result cannot be
regarded as an unreasonable ambition; for, though all
mankind were well fed, well clothed, and well housed,
they might still be half civilized.

According to the European theory, men are divided
into classes,—some to toil and earn, others to seize and
enjoy. According to the Massachusetts theory, all are to
have an equal chance for earning, and equal security in
the enjoyment of what they earn. The latter tends to
equality of condition; the former, to the grossest in-
equalities. Tried by any Christian standard of morals,
or even by any of the better sort of heathen standards,
can any one hesitate, for a moment, in declaring which
of the two will produce the greater amount of human
welfare, and which, therefore, is the more conformable
to the divine will? The European theory is blind to what
constitutes the highest glory as well as the highest duty of
a State. . . .

Our ambition as a State should trace itself to a different origin, and propose to itself a different object. Its
flame should be lighted at the skies. Its radiance and its
warmth should reach the darkest and the coldest of abodes
of men. It should seek the solution of such problems as
these: To what extent can competence displace pauperism? How nearly can we free ourselves from the low-
minded and the vicious, not by their expatriation, but
by their elevation? To what extent can the resources and
powers of Nature be converted into human welfare, the
peaceful arts of life be advanced, and the vast treasures
of human talent and genius be developed? How much
of suffering, in all its forms, can be relieved? or, what is
better than relief, how much can be prevented? Cannot
the classes of crimes be lessened, and the number of
criminals in each class be diminished? . . .

Now two or three things will doubtless be admitted to
be true, beyond all controversy, in regard to Massachusetts. By its industrial condition, and its business operations, it is exposed, far beyond any other State in the
Union, to the fatal extremes of overgrown wealth and

desperate poverty. Its population is far more dense than that of any other State. It is four or five times more dense than the average of all the other States taken together; and density of population has always been one of the proximate causes of social inequality. According to population and territorial extent there is far more capital in Massachusetts—capital which is movable, and instantaneously available—than in any other State in the Union; and probably both these qualifications respecting population and territory could be omitted without endangering the truth of the assertion. . . .

Now surely nothing but universal education can counterwork this tendency to the domination of capital and the servility of labor. If one class possesses all the wealth and the education, while the residue of society is ignorant and poor, it matters not by what name the relation between them may be called: the latter, in fact and in truth, will be the servile dependents and subjects of the former. But, if education be equally diffused, it will draw property after it by the strongest of all attractions; for such a thing never did happen, and never can happen, as that an intelligent and practical body of men should be permanently poor. Property and labor in different classes are essentially antagonistic; but property and labor in the same class are essentially fraternal. The people of Massachusetts have, in some degree, appreciated the truth that the unexampled prosperity of the State—its comfort, its competence, its general intelligence and virtue—is attributable to the education, more or less perfect, which all its people have received; but are they sensible of a fact equally important, —namely, that it is to this same education that two-thirds of the people are indebted for not being to-day the vassals of as severe a tyranny, in the form of capital, as the lower classes of Europe are bound to in any form of brute force?

Education then, beyond all other devices of human origin, is a great equalizer of the conditions of men,—the balance wheel of the social machinery. I do not here mean that it so elevates the moral nature as to make men disdain and abhor the oppression of their fellow men. This idea pertains to another of its attributes. But I mean that it gives each man the independence and the means by which he can resist the selfishness of other men. It does better than to disarm the poor of their hostility toward the rich: it prevents being poor. Agrarianism is the revenge of poverty against wealth. The wanton destruction of the property of others—the burning of hay-ricks, and corn-ricks, the demolition of machinery because it supersedes hand-labor, the sprinkling of vitriol on rich dresses —is only agrarianism run mad. Education prevents both the revenge and the madness. On the other hand, a fellow-feeling for one's class or caste is the common instinct of hearts not wholly sunk in selfish regard for a person or for a family. The spread of education, by enlarging the cultivated class or caste, will open a wider area over which the social feelings will expand; and, if this education should be universal and complete, it would do more than all things else to obliterate factitious distinctions in society. . . .

For the creation of wealth, then,—for the existence of a wealthy people and a wealthy nation,—intelligence is the grand condition. The number of improvers will increase as the intellectual constituency, if I may so call it, increases. In former times, and in most parts of the world even at the present day, not one man in a million has ever had such a development of mind as made it possible for him to become a contributor to art or science. . . . Let this development proceed, and contributions . . . of inestimable value, will be sure to follow. That political economy, therefore, which busies itself about capital and labor, supply and demand, interests and rents, favorable and unfavorable balances of trade, but leaves out of account the elements of a wide-spread mental development, is naught but stupendous folly. The greatest of all the arts in political economy is to change a consumer into a producer; and the next greatest is to increase the producing power,—and this to be directly obtained by increasing his intelligence. For mere delving, an ignorant man is but little better than a swine, whom he so much resembles in his appetites, and surpasses in his power of mischief. . . .

MASSACHUSETTS COMPULSORY SCHOOL LAW, 1852 [40]

The trouble with most of the legislation providing for public education—or placing upon towns responsibility for public education—was that the legislation was not enforced. In 1850 the Massachusetts General Court gave authority to the towns to deal with truants between the ages of 6 and 16, but not until two years later did it enact what was the first compulsory school law in the country. Even this law, however, contented itself with a requirement of twelve weeks schooling for children between the ages of 8 and 14.

✓   ✓   ✓

AN ACT CONCERNING THE ATTENDANCE OF CHILDREN AT SCHOOL

Be it enacted by the Senate and House of Representatives in General Court assembled, and by the authority of the same, as follows:

Sect. 1. Every person who shall have any child under his control, between the ages of eight and fourteen years, shall send such child to some public school within the town or city in which he resides, during at least twelve weeks, if the public schools within such town or city shall be so long kept, in each and every year during which such child shall be under his control, six weeks of which shall be consecutive.

Sect. 2. Every person who shall violate the provisions of the first section of this act shall forfeit, to the use of

[40] From "Acts and Resolves Passed by the General Court of Massachusetts, 1852" in E. W. Knight and C. L. Hall, *Readings in American Educational History* (New York, 1951) 365.

such town or city, a sum not exceeding twenty dollars, to be recovered by complaint or indictment.

Sect. 3. It shall be the duty of the school committee in the several towns or cities to inquire into all cases of violation of the first section of this act, and to ascertain of the persons violating the same, reasons, if any, for such violation, and they shall report such cases, together with such reasons, if any, to the town or city in their annual report; but they shall not report any cases such as are provided for by the fourth section of this act.

Sect. 4. If, upon inquiry by the school committee, it shall appear, or if upon the trial of any complaint or indictment under this act it shall appear, that such child has attended some school, not in the town or city in which he resides, for the time required by this act, or has been otherwise furnished with the means of education for a like period of time, or has already acquired those branches of learning which are taught in common schools, or if it shall appear that his bodily or mental condition has been such as to prevent his attendance at school, or his acquisition of learning for such a period of time, or that the person having the control of such child, is not able, by reason of poverty, to send such child to school, or to furnish him with the means of education, then such person shall be held not to have violated the provisions of this act.

— Reading No. 41 —

THE CONSTITUTION OF A LYCEUM, 1829 [41]

It was inevitable that the reformers, especially the Transcendentalist reformers, should have interested them-

[41] From *Old South Leaflets,* (Boston, n.d.) No. 139.

selves in what we now call adult education. The lyceum movement was inaugurated by Josiah Holbrook, a graduate of Yale College who had had considerable experience with agricultural education, and who published in 1826 a notable article on "Associations of Adults for Mutual Education." The idea of lyceums in villages and towns—and even in larger cities like Boston and Brooklyn—speedily caught on; by 1835 the number was estimated at three thousand. In the beginning primarily scientific, the lyceums soon attracted lecturers on religious, political, literary, and social questions: Emerson, Parker, Phillips, Greeley and others were famous Lyceum lecturers in their day. We give here an ideal Constitution of a Lyceum as drawn up by Holbrook.

✔   ✔   ✔

THE CONSTITUTION OF A LYCEUM
1829

CONSTITUTION

Many Lyceums have adopted the following or similar articles for their Constitution:—

1. The objects of the Lyceum are the improvement of its members in useful knowledge and the advancement of Popular Education.

2. To effect these objects, they will hold meetings for reading, conversation, discussions, dissertations, illustrating the sciences, or other exercises which shall be thought expedient, and, as it is found convenient, will procure a cabinet consisting of books, apparatus for illustrating the sciences, plants, minerals, and other natural or artificial productions.

3. Any person may be Member of the Lyceum by paying into the treasury annually Two Dollars; and Twenty Dollars paid at any one time will entitle a person, his or her heirs or assigns, to one membership forever. Persons under eighteen years of age will be entitled to all the privileges of the Society, except voting, for one-half the annual sum above named. . . .

5. The delegates will meet delegates from other branches of the Lyceum in this county semi-annually, to adopt regulations for their general and mutual benefit, or to take measures to introduce uniformity and improvements

into common schools, and to diffuse useful and practical knowledge generally through the community, particularly to form and aid a BOARD OF EDUCATION.

6. To raise the standard of common education, and to benefit the juvenile members of the Lyceum, a portion of the books procured shall be fitted to young minds; and teachers of schools may be permitted to use for the benefit of their pupils who are members of the Lyceum the apparatus and minerals under such restrictions as the association shall prescribe. . . .

RECOMMENDATIONS

The undersigned hereby express their opinion that popular education would be greatly advanced by measures to concentrate the views and efforts of those disposed to act in its behalf to different parts of the country.

That the formation of a Society would be the most direct and efficient measure to concentrate such views and efforts.

That the institution denominated the AMERICAN LYCEUM embraces in its plan the important objects of a National Society, for the advancement of popular education.

That it is highly desirable that an auxiliary to this Society, or a branch Lyceum should be established in every town.

That some simple articles of apparatus are important to render Lyceums interesting, useful, and permanent, and that the articles proposed by MR. HOLBROOK are fitted to this object, and that a portion of them would be useful in district and other schools.

That a weekly meeting of teachers for using apparatus, and other exercises in relation to their schools, would have a tendency to raise their qualifications and to increase the value of their services.

ELIZABETH PEABODY: RECORD OF, MR. ALCOTT'S SCHOOL, 1835 [42]

Before Bronson Alcott launched the ill-fated Fruitlands experiment (see Reading No. 8) he had devoted his energies and thought to teaching. Deeply dissatisfied with current teaching practices and malpractices, he tried to make the schoolroom a place of beauty and of happiness, foster a friendly and intimate relationship between teacher and children, abolish corporal punishment, and teach the young to think and to learn for themselves. In 1834 he opened a school at the Masonic Temple in Boston to put these principles into effect. His assistant was the eager young Elizabeth Peabody who was herself to have a long and distinguished career as an educational pioneer. The Temple School was forced to close because Alcott affronted the Victorian sensibilities of Bostonians by explaining that "A mother suffers when she has a child. When she is going to have a child she gives up her body to God, and he works upon it, in a mysterious way, and with her aid brings forth the Child's Spirit in a little Body of its own." Miss Peabody kept a record of the Temple School and in 1835 published it anonymously; later it appeared under her own name.

✓ ✓ ✓

Mr Alcott reopened his school in Boston, after four years' interval, September, 1834, at the Masonic Temple.

Conceiving that the objects which meet the senses every day for years must necessarily mold the mind,

[42] From Elizabeth Peabody, *The Record of a School, Exemplifying the General Principles of Spiritual Culture* (Boston, 1835) 10 ff.

he chose a spacious room, and ornamented it, not with such furniture as only an upholsterer can appreciate, but with such forms as would address and cultivate the imagination and heart.

In the four corners of the room, therefore, he placed, upon pedestals, busts of Socrates, Shakspeare, Milton, and Scott; and on a table, before the large Gothic window by which the room is lighted, the Image of Silence, "with his finger up, as though he said, Beware." Opposite this window was his own desk, whose front is the arc of a circle. On this he placed a small figure of a child aspiring. Behind was a very large bookcase, with closets below, a black tablet above, and two shelves filled with books. A fine cast of Christ in basso-relievo, fixed into this bookcase, is made to appear to the scholars just over the teacher's head. The bookcase itself is surmounted with a bust of Plato.

On the northern side of the room, opposite the door, was the table of the assistant, with a small figure of Atlas bending under the weight of the world. On a small bookcase behind the assistant's chair were placed figures of a child reading and a child drawing. Some old pictures, one of Harding's portraits, and several maps were hung on the walls.

The desks for the scholars, with conveniences for placing all their books in sight, and with black tablets hung over them, which swing forward when they wish to use them, are placed against the wall round the room, that when in their seats for study no scholar need look at another. On the right hand of Mr. Alcott is a sofa for the accommodation of visitors, and a small table with a pitcher and bowl. Great advantages arise from this room, every part of which speaks the thoughts of Genius. It is a silent reproach upon rudeness.

About twenty children came the first day. They were all under ten years of age, excepting two or three girls. I became his assistant, to teach Latin to such as might desire to learn.

Mr. Alcott sat behind his desk, and the children were placed in chairs in a large arc around him; the chairs so far apart that they could not easily touch each other. He then asked each one separately what idea he or she had of the purpose of coming to school. To learn, was the first answer. To learn what? By pursuing this question, all the common exercises of the school were brought up by the children themselves; and various subjects of arts, science, and philosophy. Still Mr. Alcott intimated that this was not all; and at last some one said, "To behave well;" and in pursuing this expression into its meanings, they at last agreed that they came to learn to feel rightly, to think rightly, and to act rightly. A boy of seven years old suggested that the most important of these three was right action.

Simple as all this seems, it would hardly be believed what an evident exercise it was to the children, to be led of themselves to form and express these conceptions and few steps of reasoning. Every face was eager and interested. From right actions, the conversation naturally led into the means of bringing them out. And the necessity of feeling in earnest, of thinking clearly, and of school discipline, was talked over. School discipline was very carefully considered; both Mr. Alcott's duty, and the children's duties, also various means of producing attention, self-control, perseverance, faithfulness. Among these means, correction was mentioned; and, after a consideration of its nature and issues, they all agreed that it was necessary, and that they preferred Mr. Alcott should correct them rather than leave them in their faults, and that it was his duty to do so. Various punishments were mentioned, and hurting the body was admitted to be necessary and desirable whenever words were found insufficient to command the memory of conscience. . . .

When children are committed to his charge very young, the first discipline to which he puts them is of the eye, by making them familiar with pictures. The art of Drawing has well been called the art of learning to see; and perhaps no person ever began to learn to draw, without astonishment at finding how imperfectly he had always been seeing. He finds that the most common forms are not only very falsely defined on his sense, but a vast deal that is before the eyes is entirely overlooked. . . .

The forms of things are God's address to the human soul. They are the first incitements to activity of mind; or, to speak more accurately, they are the first supporters of that activity which is the nature of the mind, and which can only be checked by the soul's being starved of Nature.

It is from considerations of this kind that Mr. Alcott very early presents to children pictured forms of things; and he selects them in the confidence that the general character of these forms will do much toward setting the direction of the current of activity, especially if we attend to and favor those primal sympathies with which Nature seems to wed different minds to different portions of the universe. But the practice of the eye in looking at forms, and that of the hand in imitating them, should be simultaneous. Mr. Alcott thinks the slate and pencil, or the chalk and blackboard, can hardly be given too early. The latter is even better than the former; for children should have free scope, as we find that their first shapings are usually gigantic. And is it not best that they should be so? Miniature, when it appears first in the order of development, seems to be always the effect of checked spirit or some artificial influence.

With such education of the eye, as a preliminary, reading and writing are begun simultaneously; and the former will be very much facilitated, and the latter come to perfection, in a much shorter time than by the usual mode. By copying print, which does not require such a sweep of hand as the script character, a clear image of each letter is gradually fixed in the mind; and while the graceful curves of the script are not attained till afterwards, yet they are attained quite as early as by the common method of beginning with them; and the clearness and distinctness of print is retained in the script, which, from being left to form itself so freely, becomes also characteristic of each individual's particular mind.

— Reading No. 43 —

WALT WHITMAN ON THE FAULTS OF PUBLIC SCHOOLS, 1847 [43]

Testimony to the failings of public schools in this generation is so voluminous and so eloquent, that we might well wonder how any pupils managed to learn anything. Teachers, it was alleged, were ill-prepared; books were ragged and almost worthless; facilities were unfit for human use. Above all, corporal punishment was looked upon as the only way to keep discipline. One of Alcott's most daring innovations was the abandonment of corporal punishment. We do not ordinarily think of Whitman as a reformer, yet he was, in his earlier days, much concerned with some aspects of social and humanitarian reform. Here is an editorial from the Brooklyn Daily Eagle *on the Seminaries of Brooklyn.*

✓   ✓   ✓

As a general thing the faults of our public schools system are—crowding too many students together, insufficiency of books, and their cost being taxed directly on the pupil—and the flogging system, which in a portion of the schools still holds its wretched sway. With pride we unite in the numerous commendations of the grand free school system of this State—with its twelve thousand seminaries, and its twenty thousand teachers, to whom each child, rich or poor, can come without money and without price! But we are none the less aware that the prodigious sum—hundreds of thousands of dollars—an-

[43] From Walt Whitman, "Free Seminaries of Brooklyn," *The Brooklyn Eagle,* Feb. 4, 1847, in Cleveland Rodgers and John Black, eds., *The Gathering of the Forces,* by Walt Whitman (New York, Putnam's, 1920) 138-41.

nually expended on these schools, might be expended to more profit. We have by no means ascended to the height of the great argument of education. The monotonous *old* still resists the fresh philosophical *new*. Form and precedent often are more thought of than reality. What are mere "order" or "learning lessons," or all the routine of the simple *outside* of school-keeping?— Absolutely nothing, in themselves; and only valuable, as far as they help the higher objects of educating the child. To teach the child *book grammar* is nothing; to teach him by example, by practice, by thoroughly clarifying the principles of correct syntax, *how to talk and write harmoniously,* is every thing. To put him through the arithmetic is not much; to make him able to compare, calculate, and quickly seize the bearings of a practical figure-question such as occurs in business every hour, is a good deal. Mere atlas geography is a sham, too, unless the learner have the position of places in his mind, and *know* the direction, distances, bearings, etc., of the countries, seas, cities, rivers and mountains, whose names (as our miserable school geographies give them,) he runs over so glibly. We care very little indeed for—what is the pride of many teachers' hearts—the military discipline of their schools, and the slavish obedience of their pupils to the imperial nod or waved hand of the master. As to the flogging plan, it is the most wretched item yet left of the ignorance and inefficiency of school-keeping. It has surrounded the office, (properly one of the noblest on earth,) with a character of contemptibleness and petty malignance, that will stick to it as long as whipping sticks among teachers' habits. What nobleness can reside in a man who catches boys by the collar and cuffs their ears? What elevation or dignity of character can even a child's elastic thoughts connect with one who cuts him over the back with a ratan or makes him hold out his hand to receive the whack of a ferule? For teachers' own sakes —for the true height and majesty of their office, hardly second to the priesthood—they should one and all unite in precluding this petty and foolish punishment—this degrader and bringerdown of their high standing. As things are, the word school-teacher is identified with a dozen unpleasant and ridiculous associations—a sour face, a whip, hard knuckles snapped on tender heads, no

gentle, fatherly kindness, no inciting of young ambition
in its noble phases, none of the beautifiers of authority,
but all that is small, ludicrous, and in after life productive of indignation. We have reason to think that the
flogging system still prevails in several of our Brooklyn
schools to quite a wretched extent. In the school in
Baltic St. under a former management, forty children
in the boys' department were thrashed in the course of
one morning! and in the female department a little girl
was so cut and marked with the ratan over back, neck
and shoulders, for some trifling offence, that the livid
marks remained there for several days! This is a pretty
fact for the character of our public seminaries! Justice to
the mass of the teachers, however, demands that they
should not be confounded with these ultra and repulsive
cases. In general, doubtless, they whip with moderation
—if that word may be applied to such a punishment at all.
Nor do we mean to impugn their motives altogether.
They think they are doing right. So did the Spanish
torturers in Peru—inquisitors in Spain—and the learned
doctors who denounced Jenner.

VIII

HUMANITARIANISM

— Reading No. 44 —

PROTEST AGAINST IMPRISONMENT FOR DEBT, 1830[44]

" From (a) "Address of the City and County Convention
    of the Workingmen's Party, July 10, 1830," in J. R.
    Commons, *et al.,* eds. *Documentary History of American
    Industrial Society,* V, 121. (b) The Poems of John
    Greenleaf Whittier, v. d.

In the United States, as in England, debtors were thrown into prison and left there until their debt was discharged. Debtors were customarily treated worse than criminals, for while the State fed and clothed and sheltered ordinary criminals, the hapless men and women imprisoned for debt were supposed to feed and clothe themselves. Conditions in all prisons were bad; those in debtors' prisons were particularly bad. Legislation ameliorating the lot of the hapless debtors came in the second decade of the century, but abolition of imprisonment for debt was slow. While most of the new western states prohibited such imprisonment in their Constitutions, eastern states were rejecting bills and constitutional amendments abolishing imprisonment for debt as late as the 1850's. We give here a protest from the Workingmen's Party of New York, and a poem by Whittier.

✓   ✓   ✓

A. Protest of the Workingmen's Party, 1830

There is one more subject to which we wish to call your attention, before we close this address. It is the subject of imprisonment for debt; it is one in which all who have a regard for the rights of their fellow men will unite, and all whose bosoms glow with philanthropy, will rejoice to see its abolition. How long fellow citizens, shall the fair page of our history be blemished by this foul blot? How long shall it be the policy of our government, to add oppression and insult to the wounded feeling of the unfortunate man? The existing laws on this subject are very defective. The creditor is not rightly protected against the swindler, and the poor man is burthened with the expense to procure bail, &c., to get through. We say the creditor is not protected, because he is at all times made to prove that the applicant has property. We would have that every man, when he contracts a debt, should make it appear that he is solvent, (if the creditor should require it) and that such declaration should be used as evidence against him, and that the court should not allow the applicant, in account for loss actually sustained, any extravagant living, horse and gig hire, &c., only allowing him to account for reasonable wearing apparel and other reasonable domestic expenses and

actual losses. If such were the case, there would be but
a limited number of applicants for the benefit of the in-
solvent laws. The industrious trader and working man
would not be so often robbed of their substance, to keep
in idleness the host of swindlers and knaves that now
prey upon their very vitals.

B.

THE PRISONER FOR DEBT

. . . . . .
What has the gray-haired prisoner done?
Has murder stained his hands with gore?
Not so; his crime's a fouler one;
GOD MADE THE OLD MAN POOR!
For this he shares a felon's cell,—
The fittest earthly type of hell!
For this, the boon for which he poured
His young blood on the invader's sword,
And counted light the fearful cost—
His blood-gained liberty is lost!

. . . . . .
Down with the LAW that binds him thus!
Unworthy freeman, let it find
No refuge from the withering curse
Of God and human kind!
Open the prison's living tomb,
And usher from its brooding gloom
The victims of your savage code
To the free sun and air of God;
No longer dare as crime to brand
The chastening of the Almighty's hand.

JOHN GREENLEAF WHITTIER

— Reading No. 45 —

EDWARD LIVINGSTON: CODE OF REFORM AND PRISON DISCIPLINE, 1824, 1833 [45]

After a short term as mayor of New York, Edward Livingston moved to New Orleans, practiced law, and was elected to the lower house of the state legislature. At the request of the legislature he undertook to prepare a system of penal law for the state. The labor of five years resulted in an elaborate series of codes: a Code of Crimes and Punishments, Code of Procedure, Code of Evidence, and Code of Reform and Prison Discipline; to each of these Livingston attached a formal Report. The whole constituted the most impressive contribution to codification, or to penal and prison reform, to come out of New York, and won for Livingston an international fame. Louisiana was too timid to adopt the new penal and prison code, but its influence was felt throughout the United States and in the states of Europe and South America as well. Livingston himself soon went to the U. S. Senate; then became Secretary of State to Jackson, and eventually Minister to France. We give here excerpts on the responsibility to educate criminals, and on the School of Reform for juvenile offenders.

✓   ✓   ✓

It is no unimportant part of this plan, that education and intellectual improvement, as well as mere physical enjoyments, are held out as inducements for the exercise of industry, skill and good conduct. These are to be rewarded by the use of books combining entertainment

[45] From Edward Livingston, *A Code of Reform and Prison Discipline, to which is Prefixed an Introductory Report to the same. . . .* (New York, 1872) 52-4, 60-64, 76-7.

with instruction; the instruments and other means of exercising the mind in science, or the hand in the delicate operations of the fine arts, of developing talent or improving skill. Such pursuits offer, perhaps, the most efficient means of reformation; they operate by reconciling the convict to himself, which is the first and most difficult point to be gained. The daily exercise of mental powers, the consciousness of progress in useful knowledge, must raise him in his own estimation; and this honest pride, once set at work, will do more to change the conduct and purify the heart, then any external agency, however constantly or skillfully applied.

Let it not be said that this is a theory too refined to be adapted to depraved and degraded convicts. Convicts are men. The most depraved and degraded are men; their minds are moved by the same springs that give activity to those of others; they avoid pain with the same care, and pursue pleasure with the same avidity, that actuate their fellow-mortals. It is the false direction only of these great motives that produces the criminal actions which they prompt. To turn them into a course that will promote the true happiness of the individual, by making them cease to injure that of society, should be the great object of penal jurisprudence. The error, it appears to me, lies in considering them as beings of a nature so inferior as to be incapable of elevation, and so bad as to make any amelioration impossible; but crime is the effect principally of intemperance, idleness, ignorance, vicious associations, irreligion, and poverty,—not of any defective natural organization; and the laws which permit the unrestrained and continual exercise of these causes are themselves the sources of those excesses which legislators, to cover their own inattention or indolence or ignorance, impiously and falsely ascribe to the Supreme Being, as if he had created man incapable of receiving the impressions of good. Let us try the experiment, before we pronounce that even the degraded convict cannot be reclaimed. It has never yet been tried. Every plan hitherto offered is manifestly defective, because none has contemplated a complete system, and partial remedies never can succeed. It would be a presumption, of which the reporter's deep sense of his own incapacity renders him incapable, were he to say that what he offers is a perfect system, or to think that it will produce all the effects which might be expected from a good one; but he may be permitted, perhaps, to believe, that the principles on which it is founded are not discordant; that it has a unity of design, and embraces a greater combination of provisions, all tending to produce the same result, than any that has yet been practised. Whether these principles are correct, or the details proper to enforce them, the superior wisdom of the legislature must determine. But to think that the best plan which human sagacity could devise will produce reformation in every case, that there will not be numerous exceptions to its general effect, would be to indulge the visionary belief of a moral panacea, applicable to all vices and all crimes; and although this would be quackery in legislation, as absurd as any that has appeared in medicine, yet, to say that there are no general rules by which reformation of the mind may be produced, is as great and fatal an error as to assert that there are in the healing art no usefull rules for preserving the general health and bodily vigor of the patient. . . .

One other institution remains to be described; one of perhaps quite as much importance as any other in the system. It is the School of Reform; designed for the confinement, and discipline, and instruction of juvenile offenders and young vagrants. Of all the establishments suggested by charity, and executed by the active and enlightened benevolence of modern times, none interests more deeply the best feelings of the heart. . . .

The place for the confinement of juvenile offenders . . . is to be considered more as a school of instruction than a prison for degrading punishment; a school in which the vicious habits of the pupil require a strict discipline, but still a school, into which he enters a vicious boy, and from which he is to depart a virtuous and industrious youth; where the involuntary vices and crimes with which his early childhood was stained are to be eradicated, their very remembrance lost; and in their place, the lessons inculcated, and the examples given, which would have guided him, had the duties of nature and society been performed. From hence he begins his career of life; and as it would be unjust to load him, on his outset, with the opprobrium which would be inseparable from an association, in the same place of punishment, with hardened offenders, it became necessary, as well from this circumstance as from the different nature of the discipline, to separate this entirely, both by locality and name, from the other prisons.

To argue the utility, or to descant on the humanity, of this establishment, after demonstrating its justice, would be a useless task. Every mind that has investigated the causes and progress of crime must acknowledge the one; every benevolent heart must feel the other. And even economy, cold, calculating economy, after stating the account in dollars and cents, must confess that this is a money saving institution. If it is wise to prevent an hundred atrocious crimes by removing the opprobrium of a venial fault, and substituting instruction for punishment; if it is the highest species of humanity to relieve from the misery of vice and the degradation of crime, to extend the operation of charity to the mind, and to snatch with its angel arm innocence from seduction; if it be a saving to society to support an infant for a few years at school, and thereby avoid the charge of the depredations of a felon for the rest of his life, and the expense of his future convictions and confinements, then is the School of Reform a wise, a humane, and an economical institution. . . .

If we mean to guard the community from the inroads of crime, every avenue must be defended. A besieged city, fortified on one side, leaving the others open to hostile attacks, would be a just image of a country in which laws are made to eradicate offenses by punishments only while they invite them by neglect of education, by the toleration of mendicity, idleness, vagrancy, and the corrupting association of the accused before trial, as well as after conviction. Yet such is the lamentable state of criminal jurisprudence, that all nations are more or less in this state. Here great severity is used to punish offenses, but no means are provided to prevent them; there mild punishments and a reformatory discipline are applied after judgment; but severe imprisonment and contaminating associations are indiscriminately inflicted on the innocent and on the guilty before trial. Between some States the contest seems which shall raise the greatest revenue from the labor of the convicts; in others the object is to degrade and make them feel their misery. Nowhere has a system been established consisting of a connected series of institutions founded on the same principle of uniformity, directed to the same end; nowhere is criminal jurisprudence treated as a science; what goes by that name, consists of a collection of dissimilar, unconnected, sometimes conflicting expedients to punish different offenses as they happen to prevail; or experiments directed by no principle to try the effect of different penalties; of permanent laws to repress temporary evils; of discretionary power, sometimes with the blindest confidence vested in the judge, and at others with the most criminal negligence given to an officer of executive justice. All these and other incongruities would cease, were the lawgiver to form correct principles; enounce them for his own guidance and that of his successors; and with them constantly before his eyes, arrange his system of criminal jurisprudence into its natural divisions, by providing for the poor, employing the idle, educating the ignorant, defining offenses and designating their correspondent punishment, regulating the mode of procedure for preventing crimes and prosecuting offenders, and giving precise rules for the government and discipline of prisons.

— Reading No. 46 —

TEMPERANCE AND PROHIBITION LEGISLATION, 1850-55 [46]

One of the most spectacular, if not one of the most effective, reform movements of this generation was

[46] From John Bach McMaster, *History of the People of the United States, from the Revolution to the Civil War,* (New York, D. Appleton and Co., 1913) VIII, 126 ff.

*directed against the ubiquitous intemperance. The first
American temperance society had been organized as early
as 1808, but it was not until the 'twenties that temperance
agitation became widespread, and not for yet another
decade that the movement became successful. By 1834
it was estimated that some 5000 temperance societies
had pledged one million persons to temperance. Gradually
it was felt that temperance was not enough, and in
the 'forties the so-called Washingtonian societies substituted total abstinence for mere temperance. It was
natural that the total abstinence—or teetotal—people
should turn to state legislatures for help, for the only
way really to assure abstinence was to prohibit the
manufacture or sale of spirituous liquors. A beginning
was made of this in the 'forties, but it was the Maine
Law of 1851 that inaugurated the short-lived prohibition
experiment. Most prohibition legislation is immensely
detailed and confusing, and instead of citing sections of
various state laws we give here John Bach McMaster's
comprehensive summary of state prohibition legislation.*

✓   ✓   ✓

The chief provisions of this famous act (the Maine
Liquor Law) were that no person should manufacture
or sell directly or indirectly any spirituous or intoxicating
liquor. But the Selectmen of any town or the Mayor and
Aldermen of any city might, annually, on the first Monday in May, appoint a suitable agent to sell spirits, wines,
or liquors for medicinal and mechanical uses and for no
other. If three voters complained on oath before a justice
of the peace or judge of a municipal or police court
that they believed liquors were kept, or deposited and intended for sale, by any person not authorized, the justice
or the judge must issue a warrant of search, and the
sheriff or constable must search the store, shop, ware-
house, or building, and, if liquor were found, seize and
destroy it, but no dwelling could be searched unless
liquor had been sold therein.

The victory was a great one, and a craze for temperance legislation swept the country from Maine to Minnesota. . . . Vermont forbade the manufacture and
sale of liquor save for chemical or manufacturing purpose
or for use at the Lord's Supper, and prohibited any

person to buy, sell, or suffer his clerk, servant, or agent to give away any spirituous liquor or mixed drink. A bill framed on the Maine model was adopted by Rhode Island and went into force on the third Monday in July. During the fortnight preceding that day the demand for liquor was so great that many a dealer sold more than he had ever before disposed of in a twelvemonth. As the hour when tippling must stop approached men hurried through the streets with demijohns and jugs, the rich stocked their cellars, and the poor spent all their money for liquor. Should the law be enforced at Newport the summer trade, it was feared, would be ruined. Thousands of the votaries of fashion, it was said, came there every August. But these, because of the despotic Maine law, would shun Newport and go to the White Mountains. The town meeting, therefore, sought to evade the law and show contempt for it by appointing as common informer a man who was nearly blind and was a spiritualist. But the work of informing was taken up by an ardent temperance man, and the proprietors of the United States Hotel and oi the Ocean House were soon under bonds to appear for trial, and five barrels of liquor and three kegs marked "lard" consigned to the Exchange Hotel, in Providence, were seized at the Stonington depot. Hotel proprietors then formed a defensive alliance to fight the laws, and the case of Green *vs.* Briggs *et al.* was soon before the United States Circuit Court for Rhode Island on a writ of replevin to recover liquor entrusted to Briggs as constable to be destroyed by order of the Court of Magistrates. The Circuit Court ruled the law to be unconstitutional because the plaintiff was deprived of property by criminal prosecution, in which he could not have trial by jury without submitting to conditions the legislature had no constitutional power to impose.

The Massachusetts act went into force two days after that of Rhode Island and met with like resistance. . . . When the Marshal and a *posse* broke into a house and seized a large quantity of hidden liquor at Salem, a crowd gathered and pelted with eggs a clergyman noted for his zeal in enforcing the law. Two hundred people of Newton met and denounced the law. Watertown liquor dealers openly defied it. In some places witnesses were attacked by mobs. At Worcester the homes of two advocates of prohibition were visited by a man, and when the owners came forth to meet him each received a blow on the head.

When Connecticut passed an act for the suppression of intemperance requiring that agents for the sale of liquor for chemical and manufacturing purposes should be appointed and appropriations made by town meetings, the Democrats hoped to defeat the administration of the law by voting in each town an appropriation of six and a quarter cents. But the plan failed and the act was rigorously enforced.

In New York the struggle at the polls and before the legislature was long and bitter. At the election in the fall of 1851 the temperance question was brought into politics, and three Senators and six Assemblymen were elected on the issue. Encouraged by this success, a City Temperance Alliance was organized in New York, and the women who were leaders in the Woman's Rights movement petitioned the legislature, held a State Temperance Convention, formed a Woman's State Temperance Society, and, despite jeers, scoffs, and insults, spoke to audiences wherever they could be gathered. No woman, they held, should be wife to a confirmed drunkard. Intemperance should be good ground for divorce, and the law makers should be called on to so change the law as to permit it. Lecturers should be sent about, tracts scattered broadcast, and all means of enlightening the public should be used. For the time being their efforts were fruitless, and the Maine law was again lost in the legislature. A bill to submit it to the people did, indeed, pass the Senate at the next session, but was lost in the House.

In Pennsylvania in 1854 a Maine law was passed by a small majority and submitted to the people. The question was prohibition or license, and in a poll of three hundred thousand votes the majority against prohibition was some three thousand. . . . The Massachusetts act was now declared unconstitutional; and an attempt to pass a Maine Liquor Law was defeated in New Hampshire and Maryland.

Michigan in 1853 submitted her act to popular vote at a special election to be held in June in every township, village, and city in the State. If it received a majority vote it was to go into effect in December; if it did not it was to take effect in March, 1870. The majority in favor of the act was twenty thousand. A Wayne County Court declared it unconstitutional. The Constitution, it was held, did not authorize the submission to the people of any act for their approval or disapproval, expressly forbade the passage of an act granting licenses to sell intoxicating liquors, and expressly granted trial by jury in all penal cases, which the Maine law did not. The Supreme Court of the State was equally divided, and the law in consequence was made practically void. In the Circuits presided over by the four judges who thought it unconstitutional all cases would be decided accordingly, and, as the people who would be the complainants had no appeal, the decisions would be final. In the other circuits whose judges held the law to be constitutional the defendant in any case might appeal to the Supreme Court, where the decision would be reversed by a vote of four to three, for the judge who tried the case could not sit.

The adoption of the Maine law by Minnesota and its ratification by the people at the polls were followed by an attempt to enforce it at St. Paul, by an attack on the sheriff and his posse, by speeches to the crowd, and by a compromise which put the liquor in the hands of a third party pending an appeal to the courts. The court held that the submission of the act to popular vote was unconstitutional. The legislature was the sole law-making body. Wisconsin submitted her act to the people; those of Indiana and Iowa were set aside by the Courts, and in Virginia a committee of the legislature reported against a prohibitory liquor law and against submitting one to popular vote. Mississippi forbade the sale of liquor without license, and unless the application was signed by a majority of the legal voters of the town. The long struggle in New Hampshire ended with the enactment of a law for the suppression of drinking houses and tippling shops, and Delaware, Ohio, Illinois, joined the goodly company of prohibition States. Ohio enacted her law the year before; but it was not till the Supreme Court of the State sustained and declared it constitutional that the people in general obeyed. Then the hotel keepers in Cleveland joined in a notice to the public announcing the closing of their bars; the fashionable saloons and restaurants followed; the Mayor in a proclamation called on

venders of liquor to obey the law and the Carson League
and the police saw to it that they did. What was done in
Cleveland was done in Columbus, Chillicothe, Cincinnati,
in all the cities of Ohio.

Iowa, Michigan, Indiana, Massachusetts framed new
laws to overcome the objections of their courts; and prohibitory bills were defeated in New Jersey by the Senate,
in Illinois by the people; in New York by the veto of the
Governor. But his successor approved one which provided that all licenses should lapse on the first of May,
and the prohibitory sections should go into force on the
fourth of July. A dispute at once arose over the meaning
of this latter provision. Well-known lawyers consulted by
the Liquor Dealers' Association, the District Attorney,
and the Corporation Counsel agreed that all licenses
ended on the first of May, that after that date no more
could be issued, and that until the fourth of July liquor
might be sold without a license, like dry goods or pota-
toes, for, said they, as the prohibition against the sale
does not take effect till the fourth of July, the penalty
for violation of the prohibition cannot be in force before that time. Lawyers and judges equally well known
took the opposite view, and for a time there was great
excitement in the temperance societies, Carson Leagues,
and among the supporters of the law. After July fourth
it was rigorously enforced.

The Supreme Court of the Second District, sitting in
Brooklyn, declared the search and seizure clauses of the
act unconstitutional, and the Court of Appeals affirmed
the decision. The Supreme Court of the Eighth District
in Buffalo held that the principle of prohibition was constitutional, but the Court of Appeals reversed the decision. The Supreme Court of Delaware, on the other hand,
unanimously upheld the constitutionality of the prohibitory liquor law of that State.

— Reading No. 47 —

RELIGIOUS FREEDOM: PETITION ON BEHALF OF ABNER KNEELAND, 1838 [47]

Abner Kneeland, a Universalist clergyman, and a universal reformer, worked his way to "free-thought" and in 1831 began to present his free-thought, and other unpopular views, in his paper, the Boston Investigator. In an issue of December 20, 1833, he used language describing the birth of Jesus which was thought to be blasphemous. He was tried and convicted for blasphemy; on appeal his conviction was upheld, and he was sentenced to serve 60 days in jail. Massachusetts liberals who believed in freedom of discussion of religion protested the conviction; we give here the petition to the Governor for the remission of Kneeland's sentence; it was drawn up by W. E. Channing and Ellis Gray Loring, two of the most respected men in the state, and signed by Emerson, Parker, Garrison, Ripley, Alcott, and others of equal standing. It was, however, in vain. As Theodore Parker said, accurately, "Abner was jugged for sixty days; but he will come out as beer from a bottle, all foaming, and will make others foam."

✔   ✔   ✔

"*To his Excellency, the Governor of the Commonwealth of Massachusetts:*

"The undersigned respectfully represent, that they are informed that Abner Kneeland, of the city of Boston, has been found guilty of the crime of blasphemy, for having published, in a certain newspaper called the Boston In-

[47] From W. H. Channing, *The Life of William Ellery Channing* (Boston, 1880) 504-5.

vestigator, his disbelief in the existence of God, in the following words:—

" 'Universalists believe in a god which I do not; but believe that their god, with all his moral attributes, (aside from nature itself,) is nothing more than a chimera of their own imagination.'

"Your petitioners have learned, by an examination of the record and documents in the case, made by one of their number, that the conviction of said Kneeland proceeded on the ground above stated. For though the indictment originally included two other publications, one of a highly irreverent, and the other of a grossly indecent character, yet it appears by the report, that, at the trial, the prosecuting officer mainly relied on the sentence above quoted, and that the judge who tried the case confined his charge wholly to stating the legal construction of its terms, and the law applicable to it.

"In these circumstances, the undersigned respectfully pray that your Excellency will grant to the said Kneeland an unconditional pardon for the offence of which he has been adjudged guilty. And they ask this, not from any sympathy with the convicted individual, who is personally unknown to most or all of them; nor from any approbation of the doctrines professed by him, which are believed by your petitioners to be as pernicious and degrading as they are false; but—

"Because the punishment proposed to be inflicted is believed to be at variance with the spirit of our institutions and our age, and with the soundest expositions of those civil and religious rights which are at once founded in our nature, and guaranteed by the constitutions of the United States and this Commonwealth;

"Because the freedom of speech and the press is the chief instrument of the progress of truth and of social improvements, and is never to be restrained by legislation, except when it invades the rights of others, or instigates to specific crimes;

"Because, if opinion is to be subjected to penalties, it is impossible to determine where punishment shall stop; there being few or no opinions in which an adverse party may not see threatenings of ruin to the state;

"Because truths essential to the existence of society

must be so palpable as to need no protection from the magistrate;

"Because the assumption by government of a right to prescribe or repress opinions has been the ground of the grossest depravations of religion, and of the most grinding despotisms;

"Because religion needs no support from penal law, and is grossly dishonored by interpositions for its defence, which imply that it cannot be trusted to its own strength and to the weapons of reason and persuasion in the hands of its friends;

"Because, by punishing infidel opinions, we shake one of the strongest foundations of faith, namely, the evidence which arises to religion from the fact, that it stands firm and gathers strength amidst the severest and most unfettered investigations of its claims;

"Because error of opinion is never so dangerous as when goaded into fanaticism by persecution, or driven by threatenings to the use of secret arts;

"Because it is well known, that the most licentious opinions have, by a natural reaction, sprung up in countries where the laws have imposed severest restraint on thought and discussion;

"Because the influence of hurtful doctrines is often propagated by the sympathy which legal severities awaken towards their supporters;

"Because we are unwilling that a man, whose unhappy course has drawn on him general disapprobation, should, by a sentence of the law, be exalted into a martyr, or become identified with the sacred cause of freedom; and, lastly,

"Because we regard with filial jealousy the honor of this Commonwealth, and are unwilling that it should be exposed to reproach, as clinging obstinately to illiberal principles, which the most enlightened minds have exploded."

— Reading No. 48 —

CHARLES LORING BRACE: THE FOUNDING OF THE CHILDREN'S AID SOCIETY, 1853 [48]

What John Spargo later called "the bitter cry of the children" echoed in many ears in the early nineteenth century. As we have seen, children worked in factories ten or twelve hours a day; were assured only a minimum of schooling; their delinquencies were regarded by the law as crimes; and, in the great cities especially, they were often left to fend for themselves from even the earliest ages. Connecticut-born Charles Loring Brace had trained for the ministry, but he was early drawn away from theology into practical social work, and he made the welfare of the homeless boys of New York his special concern. He was chiefly responsible for the founding, in 1853, of the Children's Aid Society of New York, an organization which worked incessantly to protect homeless waifs, established cheap rooming houses, summer camps, and so forth.

✟   ✟   ✟

To the Public: This society has taken its origin in the deeply settled feeling of our citizens, that something must be done to meet the increasing crime and poverty among the destitute children of New York. Its objects are to help this class, by opening Sunday meetings and industrial schools, and gradually, as means shall be furnished

[48] From Charles Loring Brace, "First Circular of the Children's Aid Society," in *The Life of Charles Loring Brace* Edited by His Daughter (New York, 1894) 489-92.

by forming lodging-houses and reading-rooms for chil-dren, and by employing paid agents, whose sole busi-ness shall be to care for them.

As Christian men, we cannot look upon this great multitude of unhappy, deserted, and degraded boys and girls without feeling our responsibility to God for them. We remember that they have the same capacities, the same need of kind and good influences, and the same immortality, as the little ones in our own homes. We bear in mind that One died for them, even as for the children of the rich and the happy. Thus far, almshouses and prisons have done little to affect the evil. But a small part of the vagrant population can be shut up in our asylums; and judges and magistrates are reluctant to con-vict children, so young and ignorant that they hardly seem able to distinguish good and evil. The class increases. Immigration is pouring in its multitudes of poor for-eigners, who leave these young outcasts everywhere aban-doned in our midst. For the most part, the boys grow up utterly by themselves. No one cares for them, and they care for no one. Some live by begging, by petty pilfer-ings, by bold robbery. Some earn an honest support by peddling matches, or apples, or newspapers. Others gather bones and rags in the street to sell. They sleep on steps, in cellars, in old barns, and in markets; they hire a bed in filthy and low lodging-houses. They cannot read. They do not go to school or attend a church. Many of them have never seen the Bible. Every cunning faculty is in-tensely stimulated. They are shrewd and old in vice when other children are in leading-strings. Few influences which are kind and good ever reach the vagrant boy. And yet, among themselves, they show generous and honest traits. Kindness can always touch them.

The *girls*, too often, grow up even more pitiable and deserted. Till of late, no one has ever cared for them. They are the crosswalk sweepers, the little apple-peddlers and candy-sellers of our city; or by more questionable means they earn their scanty bread. They traverse the low, vile streets alone, and live without mother or friends, or any share in what we should call *home*. They, also, know little of God or Christ, except by name. They grow up passionate, ungoverned; with no love or kindness ever to soften the heart. We all know their short, wild life,

and the sad end. These boys and girls, it should be remembered, will soon form the great lower class of our
city. They will influence elections; they may shape the
policy of the city; they will, assuredly, if unreclaimed,
poison society all around them. They will help to form
the great multitude of robbers, thieves, and vagrants who
are now such a burden upon the law-respecting community. . . .

In view of these evils, we have formed an association
which shall devote itself entirely to this class of vagrant
children. We do not propose in any way to conflict with
existing asylums and institutions, but to render them a
hearty co-operation, and at the same time to fill a gap,
which, of necessity, they have all left. A large multitude
of children live in the city who cannot be placed in
asylums, and yet who are uncared for and ignorant and
vagrant. We propose to give to these work, and to bring
them under religious influences. A central office has been
taken, and an agent, Charles L. Brace, has been engaged
to give his whole time to efforts for relieving the wants
of this class. As means shall come in, it is designed to
district the city, so that hereafter every ward may have
its agent, who shall be a friend to the vagrant child.
"Boys' Sunday Meetings" have already been formed,
which we hope to see extended, until every quarter has
its place of preaching to boys. With these, we intend to
connect "Industrial Schools," where the great temptations
to this class, arising from *want of work*, may be removed,
and where they can learn an honest trade. Arrangements
have been made with manufacturers, by which, if we
have the requisite funds to begin, *five hundred boys* in
different localities can be supplied with paying work. We
hope, too, especially to be the means of draining the city
of these children, by communicating with farmers, manufacturers, or families in the country, who may have need
of such for employment. When homeless boys are found
by our agents, we mean to get them homes in the families
of respectable persons in the city, and to put them in the
way of an honest living. We design, in a word, to bring
humane and kindly influences to bear on this forsaken
class—to preach in various modes the Gospel of Christ
to the vagrant children of New York.

Numbers of our citizens have long felt the evils we

would remedy, but few have the leisure or the means to devote themselves personally to this work, with the thoroughness which it requires. This society, as we propose, shall be a medium through which all can, in their measure, practically help the poor children of the city. We call upon all who recognize that these are the little ones of Christ; all who believe that crime is best averted by sowing good influences in childhood; all who are the friends of the helpless, to aid us in our enterprise. We confidently hope this wide and practical movement will have its share of Christian liberality. And we earnestly ask the contributions of those able to give, to help us in carrying forward the work.

March, 1853.

— Reading No. 49 —

DOROTHEA DIX: MEMORIAL ON THE CONDITION OF THE INSANE OF MASSACHUSETTS, 1843[49]

There is no sadder chapter in the history of man's inhumanity to man than that which describes the mistreatment of the feeble-minded and the insane even in modern times. Dorothea Dix, who taught in a girls' school in Boston, and wrote sentimental books, blundered on this great crusade by accident. In 1841 she taught a Sunday School class in East Cambridge, and visiting the jail there, found insane persons kept in an unheated room. She spent the next two years investigating conditions in the jails and asylums of the state; then, in the Rev. W. E. Channing's study, composed this famous report to the

[49] From *Old South Leaflets* (Boston, n.d.) No. 148.

*legislature on what she found. The memorial produced
a profound impression. Within a short time Massachusetts provided more adequate care for its insane. Dorothea
Dix was launched on a career which lasted for fifty years,
took her into every state in the Union and every country
in western Europe, and assured her a place as one of the
great humanitarians of the nineteenth century.*

✓   ✓   ✓

Gentlemen,—I respectfully ask to present this Memorial, believing that the *cause,* which actuates to and
sanctions so unusual a movement, presents no equivocal
claim to public consideration and sympathy. Surrendering
to calm and deep convictions of duty my habitual views
of what is womanly and becoming, I proceed briefly to
explain what has conducted me before you unsolicited
and unsustained, trusting, while I do so, that the memori-
alist will be speedily forgotten in the memorial. . . .

I come to present the strong claims of suffering humanity. I come to place before the Legislature of Massachusetts the condition of the miserable, the desolate, the
outcast. I come as the advocate of helpless, forgotten,
insane, and idiotic men and women; of beings sunk to
a condition from which the most unconcerned would
start with real horror; of beings wretched in our prisons,
and more wretched in our almshouses. And I cannot suppose it needful to employ earnest persuasion, or stubborn argument, in order to arrest and fix attention upon
a subject only the more strongly pressing in its claims
because it is revolting and disgusting in its details.

I must confine myself to few examples, but am ready
to furnish other and more complete details, if required.
If my pictures are displeasing, coarse, and severe, my
subjects, it must be recollected, offer no tranquil, refined,
or composing features. The condition of human beings,
reduced to the extremest states of degradation and misery, cannot be exhibited in softened language, or adorn
a polished page.

I proceed, gentlemen, briefly to call your attention to
the *present* state of insane persons confined within this
Commonwealth, in *cages, closets, cellars, stalls, pens!
Chained, naked, beaten with rods,* and *lashed* into obedience.

As I state cold, severe *facts,* I feel obliged to refer to persons, and definitely to indicate localities. But it is upon my subject, not upon localities or individuals, I desire to fix attention; and I would speak as kindly as possible of all wardens, keepers, and other responsible officers, believing that *most* of these have erred not through hardness of heart and wilful cruelty so much as want of skill and knowledge, and want of consideration. Familiarity with suffering, it is said, blunts the sensibilities, and where neglect once finds a footing other injuries are multiplied. This is not all, for it may justly and strongly be added that, from the deficiency of adequate means to meet the wants of these cases, it has been an absolute impossibility to do justice in this matter. Prisons are not constructed in view of being converted into county hospitals, and almshouses are not founded as receptacles for the insane. And yet, in the face of justice and common sense, wardens are by law compelled to receive, and the masters of almshouses not to refuse, insane and idiotic subjects in all stages of mental disease and privation.

It is the Commonwealth, not its integral parts, that is accountable for most of the abuses which have lately and do still exist. I repeat it, it is defective legislation which perpetuates and multiplies these abuses. In illustration of my subject, I offer the following extracts from my Notebook and Journal:—

Springfield. In the jail, one lunatic woman, furiously mad, a State pauper, improperly situated, both in regard to the prisoners, the keepers, and herself. It is a case of extreme self-forgetfulness and oblivion to all the decencies of life, to describe which would be to repeat only the grossest scenes. She is much worse since leaving Worcester. In the almshouse of the same town is a woman apparently only needing judicious care, and some well-chosen employment, to make it unnecessary to confine her in solitude, in a dreary unfurnished room. Her appeals for employment and companionship are most touching, but the mistress replied "she had no time to attend to her." . . .

Concord. A woman from the hospital in a cage in the almshouse. In the jail several, decently cared for in general, but not properly placed in a prison. Violent, noisy, unmanageable most of the time.

Lincoln. A woman in a cage. *Medford.* One idiotic subject chained, and one in a close stall for seventeen years. *Pepperell.* One often doubly chained, hand and foot; another violent; several peaceable now. *Brookfield.* One man caged, comfortable. *Granville.* One often closely confined; now losing the use of his limbs from want of exercise. *Charlemont.* One man caged. *Savoy.* One man caged. *Lenox.* Two in the jail, against whose unfit condition there the jailer protests.

Dedham. The insane disadvantageously placed in the jail. In the almshouse, two females in stalls, situated in the main building; lie in wooden bunks filled with straw; always shut up. One of these subjects is supposed curable. The overseers of the poor have declined giving her a trial at the hospital, as I was informed, on account of expense.

Franklin. One man chained; decent. *Taunton.* One woman caged. *Plymouth.* One man stall-caged; from Worcester Hospital. *Scituate.* One man and one woman stall-caged. *West Bridgewater.* Three idiots. Never removed from one room. *Barnstable.* Four females in pens and stalls. Two chained certainly. I think all. Jail, one idiot. *Wellfleet.* Three insane. One man and one woman chained, the latter in a bad condition. *Brewster.* One woman violently mad, solitary. Could not see her, the master and mistress being absent, and the paupers in charge having strict orders to admit no one. *Rochester.* Seven insane; at present none caged. *Milford.* Two insane, not now caged. *Cohasset.* One idiot, one insane; most miserable condition. *Plympton.* One insane, three idiots; condition wretched.

Besides the above, I have seen many who, part of the year, are chained or caged. The use of cages all but universal. Hardly a town but can refer to some not distant period of using them; chains are less common; negligences frequent; wilful abuse less frequent than sufferings proceeding from ignorance, or want of consideration. I encountered during the last three months many poor creatures wandering reckless and unprotected through the country. Innumerable accounts have been sent me of persons who had roved away unwatched and unsearched after; and I have heard that responsible persons, controlling the almshouses, have not thought themselves culpable in sending away from their shelter, to cast upon the chances of remote relief, insane men and women. These, left on the highways, unfriended and incompetent to control or direct their own movements, sometimes have found refuge in the hospital, and others have not been traced. But I cannot particularize. In traversing the State, I have found hundreds of insane persons in every variety of circumstance and condition, many whose situation could not and need not be improved; a less number, but that very large, whose lives are the saddest pictures of human suffering and degradation. I give a few illustrations; but description fades before reality.

Danvers. November. Visited the almshouse. A large building, much out of repair. Understand a new one is in contemplation. Here are from fifty-six to sixty inmates, one idiotic, three insane; one of the latter in close confinement at all times.

Long before reaching the house, wild shouts, snatches of rude songs, imprecations and obscene language, fell upon the ear, proceeding from the occupant of a low building, rather remote from the principal building to which my course was directed. Found the mistress, and was conducted to the place which was called *"the home"* of the *forlorn* maniac, a young woman, exhibiting a condition of neglect and misery blotting out the faintest idea of comfort, and outraging every sentiment of decency. She had been, I learnt, "a respectable person, industrious and worthy. Disappointments and trials shook her mind, and, finally, laid prostrate reason and self-control. She became a maniac for life. She had been at Worcester Hospital for a considerable time, and had been returned as incurable." The mistress told me she understood that, "while there, she was comfortable and decent." Alas, what a change was here exhibited! She had passed from one degree of violence to another, in swift progress. There she stood, clinging to or beating upon the bars of her caged apartment, the contracted size of which afforded space only for increasing accumulations of filth, a *foul* spectacle. There she stood with naked arms and dishevelled hair, the unwashed frame invested with fragments of unclean garments, the air so extremely offensive, though ventilation was afforded on all sides save one, that it was not possible to remain beyond a few moments without retreating for recovery to the outward air. Irritation of body, produced by utter filth and exposure, incited her to the horrid process of tearing off her skin by inches. Her face, neck, and person were thus disfigured to hideousness. She held up a fragment just rent off. To my exclamation of horror, the mistress replied: "Oh, we can't help it. Half the skin is off sometimes. We can do nothing with her; and it makes no difference what she eats, for she consumes her own filth as readily as the food which is brought her." . . .

Men of Massachusetts, I beg, I implore, I demand pity and protection for these of my suffering, outraged sex. Fathers, husbands, brothers, I would supplicate you for this boon; but what do I say? I dishonor you, divest you at once of Christianity and humanity, does this appeal imply distrust. If it comes burdened with a doubt of your righteousness in this legislation, then blot it out; while I declare confidence in your honor, not less than your humanity. Here you will put away the cold, calculating spirit of selfishness and self-seeking; lay off the armor of local strife and political opposition; here and now, for once, forgetful of the earthly and perishable, come up to these halls and consecrate them with one heart and one mind to works of righteousness and just judgment. Become the benefactors of your race, the just guardians of the solemn rights you hold in trust. Raise up the fallen, succor the desolate, restore the outcast, defend the helpless, and for your eternal and great reward receive the benediction, "Well done, good and faithful servants, become rulers over many things!" . . .

Gentlemen, I commit to you this sacred cause. Your action upon this subject will affect the present and future condition of hundreds and of thousands.

In this legislation, as in all things, may you exercise that "wisdom which is the breath of the power of God."

Respectfully submitted,

D. L. DIX.

85 MT. VERNON STREET, BOSTON.
  January, 1843.

IX

THE PEACE CRUSADE

— Reading No. 50 —

WILLIAM LLOYD GARRISON: DECLARATION OF NON-RESISTANCE SENTIMENTS, 1838 [50]

The Napoleonic Wars and the War of 1812 led many humane men and women to consider how nations could avoid wars altogether. The first peace societies were organized by David Dodge in New York and by Noah Worcester and W. E. Channing in Massachusetts in 1815. The idea spread, and in 1828 many state societies were brought together to form the American Peace Society; this in turn co-operated with similar societies in London, Paris, and other European capitals. Just as the antiliquor crusaders had divided between those who believed in temperance and those who argued prohibition, so the peace crusaders split on the issue of non-resistance versus defensive (or in some cases "just") wars. William Lloyd Garrison, who regarded himself as a "universal reformer," was the leader of the non-resistance group. In 1838 he organized the New England Non-Resistance Society which drew up this Declaration of Sentiments.

[50] From "Declaration of Sentiments Adopted by the Peace Convention, Boston, Sept. 18, 19 and 20, 1838," in William Lloyd Garrison, *The Story of His Life, Told by His Children* (New York, 1885) II, 230-32.

✓   ✓   ✓

DECLARATION OF SENTIMENTS
ADOPTED BY THE
PEACE CONVENTION
Held in Boston, September 18, 19, & 20, 1838.

ASSEMBLED in Convention, from various sections of the American Union, for the promotion of peace on earth and good-will among men, we, the undersigned, regard it as due to ourselves, to the cause which we love, to the country in which we live, and to the world, to publish a DECLARATION, expressive of the principles we cherish, the purposes we aim to accomplish, and the measures we shall adopt to carry forward the work of peaceful, universal reformation.

We cannot acknowledge allegiance to any human government; neither can we oppose any such government by a resort to physical force. We recognize but one KING and LAWGIVER, one JUDGE and RULER of mankind. We are bound by the laws of a kingdom which is not of this world; the subjects of which are forbidden to fight; in which MERCY and TRUTH are met together, and RIGHTEOUSNESS and PEACE have kissed each other; which has no state lines, no national partitions, no geographical boundaries; in which there is no distinction of rank, or division of caste, or inequality of sex; the officers of which are PEACE, its exactors RIGHTEOUSNESS, its walls SALVATION, and its gates PRAISE; and which is destined to break in pieces and consume all other kingdoms.

Our country is the world, our countrymen are all mankind. We love the land of our nativity only as we love all other lands. The interests, rights, liberties of American citizens are no more dear to us than are those of the whole human race. Hence, we can allow no appeal to patriotism, to revenge any national insult or injury. The PRINCE OF PEACE, under whose stainless banner we rally, came not to destroy, but to save, even the worst of enemies. He has left us an example, that we should follow his steps. GOD COMMENDETH HIS LOVE TOWARD US, IN THAT WHILE WE WERE YET SINNERS, CHRIST DIED FOR US.

We conceive, that if a nation has no right to defend itself against foreign enemies, or to punish its invaders, no individual possesses that right in his own case. The unit cannot be of greater importance than the aggregate. If one man may take life, to obtain or defend his rights, the same license must necessarily be granted to communities, states, and nations. If *he* may use a dagger or a pistol, *they* may employ cannon, bomb-shells, land and naval forces. The means of self-preservation must be in proportion to the magnitude of interests at stake and the number of lives exposed to destruction. But if a rapacious and bloodthirsty soldiery, thronging these shores from abroad, with intent to commit rapine and destroy life, may not be resisted by the people or magistracy, then ought no resistance to be offered to domestic troublers of the public peace or of private security. No obligation can rest upon Americans to regard foreigners as more sacred in their persons than themselves, or to give them a monopoly of wrong-doing with impunity.

The dogma, that all the governments of the world are approvingly ordained of God, and that THE POWERS THAT BE in the United States, in Russia, in 1   ey, are in accordance with his will, is not less absur than impious. It makes the impartial Author of human freedom and equality, unequal and tyrannical. It cannot be affirmed that THE POWERS THAT BE, in any nation, are actuated by the spirit or guided by the example of Christ, in the treatment of enemies; therefore, they cannot be agreeable to the will of God; and therefore, their overthrow, by a spiritual regeneration of their subjects, is inevitable.

We register our testimony, not only against all wars, whether offensive or defensive, but all preparations for war; against every naval ship, every arsenal, every fortification; against the militia system and a standing army; against all military chieftains and soldiers; against all monuments commemorative of victory over a fallen foe, all trophies won in battle, all celebrations in honor of military or naval exploits; against all appropriations for the defence of a nation by force and arms, on the part of any legislative body; against every edict of government requiring of its subjects military service. Hence, we deem it unlawful to bear arms, or to hold a military office.

As every human government is upheld by physical strength, and its laws are enforced virtually at the point of the bayonet, we cannot hold any office which imposes upon its incumbent the obligation to compel men to do right, on pain of imprisonment or death. We therefore voluntarily exclude ourselves from every legislative and judicial body, and repudiate all human politics, worldly honors, and stations of authority. If *we* cannot occupy a seat in the legislature or on the bench, neither can we elect *others* to act as our substitutes in any such capacity.

It follows, that we cannot sue any man at law, to compel him by force to restore anything which he may have wrongfully taken from us or others; but if he has seized our coat, we shall surrender up our cloak, rather than subject him to punishment.

We believe that the penal code of the old covenant, AN EYE FOR AN EYE, AND A TOOTH FOR A TOOTH, has been abrogated by JESUS CHRIST; and that, under the new covenant, the forgiveness instead of the punishment of enemies has been enjoined upon all his disciples, in all cases whatsoever. To extort money from enemies, or set them upon a pillory, or cast them into prison, or hang them upon a gallows, is obviously not to forgive, but to take retribution. VENGEANCE IS MINE—I WILL REPAY, SAITH THE LORD.

— Reading No. 51 —

WILLIAM LADD: PROGRAM FOR A CONGRESS OF NATIONS, 1840[51]

Almost everybody was in favor of peace, in the abstract, but clearly it would not come about through moral exhortation. It was William Ladd of Maine who made

[51] From William Ladd, *An Essay on a Congress of Nations* (New York, Oxford University Press, 1916) 103-5.

the first important concrete proposals. A graduate of Harvard College who had one career as a sea-captain, and a second as a farmer, Ladd was caught up in the peace crusade early in the 1820's, and devoted the rest of his life to indefatigable labors for peace. He founded the American Peace Society and edited its journal; sustained peace organizations and propaganda with his own money, and just before his death brought together his thinking, and that of his co-workers, in this famous Essay on a Congress of Nations *(Boston, 1840). The program set forth here embraced both a congress of nations to formulate international law, and a Court of arbitration to interpret and enforce it. We give here passages from the introductory argument on the evils of war.*

✓   ✓   ✓

1. IT is a generally acknowledged principle, that nations have no moral right to go to war, until they have tried to preserve peace by every lawful and honorable means. This, the strongest advocate for war, in these enlightened days, will not deny, whatever might have been the opinion of mankind, on the subject, in darker ages. When a nation has received an injury, if it be of such a magnitude as, in the opinion of the injured party, ought not to be submitted to; the first thing to be done is to seek an explanation from the injuring nation; and it will be often found, that the injury was unintentional, or that it originated in misapprehension and mistake, or that there is no real ground of offence. Even where the ground of offence is undeniable, and, in the opinion of the world, the injured nation has a *right* to declare war, it is now generally believed, that they are not so likely to obtain redress and reparation by war as by forbearance and negotiation; and that it is their bounden duty, both to themselves and to the world at large, to exhaust every means of negotiation, before they plunge themselves and other nations into the horrors and crimes of war. The United States had much ground of complaint against Great Britain, during Washington's administration. Instead of declaring war, Jay was sent to England, and full and complete satisfaction was obtained for all the injuries received, by the influence of moral power alone, for we had not then a single ship of war on the

ocean. At a subsequent period, with twice the population, and twenty times the means of offence, impatient of a protracted negotiation, we resorted to war, and got no reparation of injuries, or satisfaction whatever, except revenge, bought at an enormous expense of men and money, and made peace, leaving every cause of complaint in the *statu quo ante bellum.* Had we protracted the negotiation thirty days longer, the war and all its evils, physical and moral, would have been avoided. Sometimes negotiations have failed altogether to obtain redress. Then an offer of arbitration should follow. Now what we are seeking for is, a regular system of arbitration, and the organization of a board of arbitrators, composed of the most able civilians in the world, acting on well-known principles, established and promulgated by a Congress of Nations. If there were such a Court, no civilized nation could refuse to leave a subject of international dispute to its adjudication. Nations have tried war long enough. It has never settled any principle, and generally leaves dissensions worse than it found them. It is, therefore, high time for the Christian world to seek a more rational, cheap, and equitable mode of settling international difficulties.

2. When we consider the horrible calamities which war has caused, the millions of lives it has cost, and the unutterable anguish which it produces, not only on the battlefield and in the military hospital, but in the social circle and the retired closet of the widow and orphan, we have reason to conclude, that the inquisition, the slave trade, slavery, and intemperance, all put together, have not caused half so much grief and anguish to mankind as war. It is the duty, therefore, of every *philanthropist,* and every *statesman,* to do what they can to support a measure which will probably prevent many a bloody war, even if the probability were but a faint one.

3. When we consider that war is the hotbed of every crime, and that it is the principal obstacle to the conversion of the heathen, and that it sends millions unprepared suddenly into eternity, every *Christian* ought to do all he can to prevent the evil in every way in his power, not only by declaiming against war, and showing its sin and folly, but by assisting to bring forward a plan which is calculated to lessen the horrors and frequency

of war. Should all the endeavors of every philanthropist, statesman and Christian in the world be successful in preventing only one war, it would be a rich reward for their labor. If only once in a century, two nations should be persuaded to leave their disputes to a Court of Nations, and thereby one war be avoided, all the expense of maintaining such a court would be repaid with interest

4. We therefore conclude, that every man, whether his station be public or private, who refuses to lend his aid in bringing forward this plan of a Congress and Court of Nations, neglects his duty to his country, to the world, and to God, and does not act consistently with the character of a statesman, philanthropist, or Christian.

— Reading No. 52 —

ELIHU BURRITT: ADDRESS ON A CONGRESS OF NATIONS, 1849[52]

When Ladd died, in 1841, leadership in the American peace movement passed to Elihu Burritt. This "learned blacksmith" who had taught himself a score of languages, and had long concerned himself with reform and education, threw his tremendous energies into making the peace movement truly international, and winning acceptance for Ladd's program of a congress of nations. In 1848 he organized the first World Conference for Peace, at Brussels, and followed this up with congresses in Paris, London, Frankfurt, and elsewhere. We give here an excerpt from Burritt's address in Paris on the idea of a Congress of Nations.

[52] From Elihu Burritt, "A Congress of Nations," address at Paris, 1849, in *Old South Leaflets* (Boston, n.d.) No. 146.

Let us suppose that (the Congress) should meet at some convenient town in Switzerland, or in some other central territory, which should be considered neutral ground, or free from any local influence which might affect its conclusions. They would immediately proceed to revise and adopt the international code, clause by clause. And clause by clause it might be transmitted to the national legislatures in session at Paris, London, Frankfort, Washington, and other capitals. At the end of six months, perhaps, the last paragraph has been elaborated and adopted by the Congress, and ratified by all the national assemblies represented in it. We have now a well-digested code, created, sanctioned, and solemnized by all the moral *prestige* and authority that can be acquired from human legislation. The august senate which constructed it was composed of delegates chosen by the representatives of the peoples. The most sublime legislative assembly that ever met on earth, they gave the result of the deliberations to their respective national assemblies for revision, amendment, and adoption. Here, again, the people took part in the enactment of this code. Here, again, they affixed to its statutes the seal of their suffrage, and it became the common law of nations, invested with all the moral authority that human legislation can give to law. On arriving at this result, we have taken the first great step in organizing peace in the society of nations. We have established a basis upon which their intercourse may be regulated by clearly defined and solemnly recognized principles of justice and equity. The next step, and of equal importance, is to constitute a permanent international tribunal, which shall interpret and apply this code in the adjudication of questions submitted to its decision. The illustrious assembly, therefore, enters upon the second department of its labors, and projects a plan for the establishment of this High Court of Nations. And this plan is adopted, also, in the same manner as the code itself. Let us suppose that it prescribes the appointment of two judges, for life or otherwise, by the government or legislature of each nation represented in the Congress. This number is suggested by the constitution of the Senate of the United States, which is composed of two delegates, elected by the legislature of every state, great or small. If it is deemed necessary that this tribunal shall immediately replace the Congress, then the latter, we will suppose, continues its sessions until the judges are appointed. Having accomplished the two great objects for which it was convoked, it is instructed to apply its attention to matters of minor international interest, until the judges arrive, to open the High Court. For instance, they digest a plan for establishing throughout the civilized world a uniformity of weights, measures, moneys, rates of postage, and for creating other facilities for the social and commercial intercourse of nations, thus preparing them for that relation to each other which should exist between the members of a vast and peaceful commonwealth. We now reach the grand consummation of our system. The High Court of Nations is opened with all the imposing solemnities befitting the occasion. Each nation, we may believe, has selected two of its most profound and eminent men to fill the seats allotted to it in this grand tribunal. Occupying the sublimest position to which the suffrage of mankind could raise them, they will act, we may presume, under a proper sense of the dignity and responsibility of their high vocation. Constituting the highest court of appeal this side of the bar of Eternal Justice, they will endeavour to assimilate their decisions, as nearly as possible, to those of unerring wisdom. Here, then, we complete the chain of universal law and order. Here we organize a system which is to connect the great circles of humanity, and regulate the mutual deportment of nations by the same principles of justice and equity as govern the intercourse of the smallest communities of men. We establish an order of society by which great nations, without deposing a single prerogative of their legitimate sovereignty, accept the condition of individuals who are amenable to law. For our system, if adopted, would not trench upon the complete independence of the different states. Neither the Congress nor the High Court of Nations would pretend to exercise any jurisdiction over the internal affairs of a country, or exert any direct political influence upon its institutions. Neither would they be designed to confederate the different states of the civilized world in a political union, like the United States of America. The great international tribunal which we

propose would not be like the Supreme Court of the
United States, to which not only the thirty little republics,
but every inhabitant of the Union, may appeal for its
decision in any case which cannot be settled by inferior
authorities. The different nations would still retain all the
prerogatives of their mutual independence. Even if dif-
ferences arose between them, they would endeavor to
settle them as before, by negotiation. But, if that medium
failed to effect an honorable and satisfactory adjustment,
they would then refer the matter in dispute to the arbitration of this High Court, which, in concert with other
nations, they had constituted for that purpose. The existence of such a last court of appeal would inevitably
facilitate the arrangement of these questions by negotiation, which is now often embarrassed and thwarted by
its dangerous proximity to an appeal to arms. Whenever
a difficulty arose between two countries, the last resort,
after negotiation had failed, would not suggest to the
mind of either party the terrible trial of the battlefield,
but the calm, impartial, and peaceful adjudication of the
High Tribunal of the Peoples. And, when once the idea of
war has been displaced in the minds of nations by the
idea of a quiet administration of justice and equity,
preparations for war, and all the policies which it requires
and creates, will gradually disappear from international
society. The different nations would soon accustom
themselves to refer their cases to this High Court of
Appeal with as much confidence as the different states
of the American Union now submit their controversies
to the decision of the Supreme Court of the United States.
On the list of cases brought before that court may be
found sometimes one entitled "New York *v.* Virginia,"
or "Pennsylvania *v.* Ohio"; and, however heavily the
verdict may bear upon one of the parties, scarcely a
murmur is heard against it. In like manner we might see
reported, among other decisions of this international
tribunal, the case of "France *v.* England," "Denmark *v.*
Prussia," or "Mexico *v.* the United States."

CHARLES SUMNER: THE TRUE GRANDEUR OF NATIONS, 1845 [53]

One of Boston's bright young men, Charles Sumner, was selected, at 34, to deliver the Independence Day Oration on July 4, 1845. Speaking to an audience of Boston gentry—including many army and navy officers —Sumner distinguished (or disgraced) himself by announcing that there was no war that was honorable, no peace that was dishonorable. For this, and for his opposition to the War with Mexico, Sumner was well-nigh ostracized by polite society, but was taken up by the reformers and antislavery elements, who helped send him to the Senate in 1851.

✦   ✦   ✦

Can there be in our age any peace that is not honorable, any war that is not dishonorable? The true honor of a nation is conspicuous only in deeds of justice and beneficence, securing and advancing human happiness. In the clear eye of that Christian judgment which must yet prevail, vain are the victories of War, infamous its spoils. He is the benefactor, and worthy of honor, who carries comfort to wretchedness, dries the tear of sorrow, relieves the unfortunate, feeds the hungry, clothes the naked, does justice, enlightens the ignorant, unfastens the fetters of the slave, and finally, by virtuous genius, in art, literature, science, enlivens and exalts the hours of life, or, by generous example, inspires a love for God and man. This is the Christian hero; this is the man of

[53] From Charles Sumner, "The True Grandeur of Nations," in *Works* (Boston, 1875) I, 9-10, 67-69.

honor in a Christian land. He is no benefactor, nor worthy of honor, whatever his worldly renown, whose life is absorbed in feats of brute force, who renounces the great law of Christian brotherhood, whose vocation is blood.
. . .

. . . There is still another influence stimulating War, and interfering with the natural attractions of Peace: I refer to a selfish and exaggerated *prejudice of country,* leading to physical aggrandizement and political exaltation at the expense of other countries, and in disregard of justice. Nursed by the literature of antiquity, we imbibe the sentiment of heathen patriotism. Exclusive love for the land of birth belonged to the religion of Greece and Rome. . . .

It is the policy of rulers to encourage this exclusive patriotism, and here they are aided by the examples of antiquity. I do not know that any one nation is permitted to reproach another with this selfishness. All are selfish. Men are taught to live, not for mankind, but only for a small portion of mankind. The pride, vanity, ambition, brutality even, which all rebuke in the individual, are accounted virtues, if displayed in the name of country. Among us the sentiment is active, while it derives new force from the point with which it has been expressed. An officer of our navy, one of the heroes nurtured by War, whose name has been praised in churches, going beyond all Greek, all Roman example, exclaimed, 'Our country, *right or wrong,*'—a sentiment dethroning God and enthroning the Devil, whose flagitious character must be rebuked by every honest heart. . . .

. . . According to the old idea, still too prevalent, man is made for the State, not the state for man. Far otherwise is the truth. The State is an artificial body, for the security of the people. How constantly do we find in human history that the people are sacrificed for the State,—to build the Roman name, to secure for England the trident of the sea, to carry abroad the conquering eagles of France! This is to barter the greater for the less,—to sacrifice humanity, embracing more even than country *all the charities of all,* for the sake of a mistaken grandeur.

Not that I love country less, but Humanity more, do I now and here plead the cause of a higher and truer patriotism. I cannot forget that we are men by a more sacred bond than we are citizens,—that we are children of a common Father more than we are Americans.

Thus do seeming diversities of nations—separated by accident of language, mountain, river, or sea—all disappear, and the multitudinous tribes of the globe stand forth as members of one vast Human Family, where strife is treason to Heaven, and all war is nothing else than *civil* war. In vain restrict this odious term, importing so much of horror, to the dissensions of a single community. It belongs also to feuds between nations. The soul trembles aghast in the contemplation of fields drenched with fraternal gore, where the happiness of homes is shivered by neighbors, and kinsman sinks beneath the steel nerved by a kinsman's hand. This is civil war, accursed forever in the calendar of Time. In the faithful record of the future, recognizing the True Grandeur of Nations, the Muse of History, inspired by a loftier justice and touched to finer sensibilities, will extend to Universal Man the sympathy now confined to country, and no war will be waged without arousing everlasting judgment.

CONCLUSION

— Reading No. 54 —

NATHANIEL HAWTHORNE: EARTH'S HOLOCAUST, 1844 [54]

We close—as we opened—with some general, philosophical observations on reform and reformers. Neither

[54] From Nathaniel Hawthorne, *Earth's Holocaust*, 1844, v. ed., v. d.

the authors nor, for that matter, the excerpts we give here
require any introduction or any gloss. It is sufficient to
note that they represent diametrically opposite points of
view. Hawthorne, in this parable written early in his lit-
erary career, views reform as primarily destructive, even
nihilistic. Greeley, who after all knew a bit more about
it from experience, concludes that though the life of the
reformer is hard, no other life is worth living at all: thus
he vindicates Emerson's aphorism, "what is man born
for but to be a reformer?" Students will doubtless sub-
scribe to one or the other of these views according to
their temperaments.

    ✓   ✓   ✓

. . . I know not whether it were the excitement of the
scene, or whether the good people around the bonfire
were really growing more enlightened every instant; but
they now proceeded to measures in the full length of
which I was hardly prepared to keep them company. For
instance, some threw their marriage certificates into the
flames, and declared themselves candidates for a higher,
holier, and more comprehensive union than that which
had subsisted from the birth of time under the form of
the connubial tie. Others hastened to the vaults of banks
and to the coffers of the rich,—all of which were open
to the first comer on this fated occasion—and brought
entire bales of paper money to enliven the blaze, and tons
of coin to be melted down by its intensity. Henceforth,
they said, universal benevolence uncoined and exhaust-
less, was to be the golden currency of the world. At this
intelligence the bankers and speculators in the stocks
grew pale, and a pickpocket, who had reaped a rich
harvest among the crowd, fell down in a deadly fainting
fit. A few men of business burned their daybooks and
ledgers, the notes and obligations of their creditors, and
all other evidences of debts due to themselves; while perhaps a somewhat larger number satisfied their zeal for
reform with the sacrifice of any uncomfortable recollec-
tion of their own indebtment. There was then a cry
that the period was arrived when the title deeds of landed
property should be given to the flames, and the whole
soil of the earth revert to the public, from whom it had
been wrongfully abstracted and most unequally distrib-

uted among individuals. Another party demanded that all written constitutions, set forms of government, legislative acts, statute books, and everything else on which human invention had endeavored to stamp its arbitrary laws, should at once be destroyed, leaving the consummated world as free as the man first created. . . .

— Reading No. 55 —

HORACE GREELEY: THE LIFE OF THE REFORMER [55]

The greatest editor of his day was also, in all probability, the most influential single figure in the world of reform. This Yankee farmboy who conquered New York, and then the whole North, was ever open-minded, tolerant, intellectually curious, resourceful, and optimistic. He lent his paper, and his enormous influence, to a dozen major reform movements—antislavery, land reform, civil service reform, temperance, and many others. At the end of his life he reviewed his own experience as a reformer, and found it rewarding.

Indeed, though the life of the Reformer may seem rugged and arduous, it were hard to say considerately that any other were worth living at all. Who can thoughtfully affirm that the career of the conquering, desolating, subjugating warrior,—of the devotee of Gold, or Pomp, or Sensual Joys; the Monarch in his purple, the Miser by his chest, the wassailer over his bowl,—is not a libel on Humanity and an offence against God? But the earnest, unselfish Reformer,—born into a state of darkness, evil,

---

[55] From Horace Greeley, "Reform and Reformers" in *Recollections of a Busy Life*, (New York, 1868) 526-7.

and suffering, and honestly striving to replace these by light, and purity, and happiness,—he may fall and die, as so many have done before him, but he cannot fail. His vindication shall gleam from the walls of his hovel, his dungeon, his tomb; it shall shine in the radiant eyes of uncorrupted Childhood, and fall in blessings from the lips of high-hearted, generous Youth. As the untimely death of the good is our strongest moral assurance of the Resurrection, so the life wearily worn out in doubtful and perilous conflict with Wrong and Woe is our most conclusive evidence that Wrong and Woe shall yet vanish forever. Luther, dying amid the agonizing tears and wild consternation of all Protestant Germany,—Columbus, borne in regal pomp to his grave by the satellites of the royal miscreant whose ingratitude and perfidy had broken his mighty heart,—Lovejoy, pouring out his life-blood beside the Press whose freedom he had so gallantly defended,—yes, and not less majestic, certainly not less tragic, than either, the lowly and lonely couch of the dying 'Uncle Tom,' whose whole life had been a brave and Christian battle against monstrous injustice and crime,—these teach us, at least, that all true greatness is ripened, and tempered, and proved, in life-long struggle against vicious beliefs, traditions, practices, institutions; and that not to have been a Reformer is not to have truly lived. Life is a bubble which any breath may dissolve; Wealth or Power a snow-flake, melting momently into the treacherous deep across whose waves we are floated on to our unseen destiny; but to have lived so that one less orphan is called to choose between starvation and infamy,—one less slave feels the lash applied in mere wantonness or cruelty,—to have lived so that some eyes of those whom Fame shall never know are brightened and others suffused at the name of the beloved one,— so that the few who knew him truly shall recognize him as a bright, warm, cheering presence, which was here for a season and left the world no worse for his stay in it,— this surely is to have really *lived*,—and not wholly in vain.

INDEX